THE BOOK OF
AMERICAN SKIING

THE BOOK OF

AMERICAN SKIING

BY EZRA BOWEN

Ski Editor of **Sports Illustrated**

Design and Layout by MARTIN NATHAN

J. B. Lippincott Company

Philadelphia and New York

This book is dedicated to Jack O'Brien, a real professional, who taught me how to work.

PREFACE

This is not a book on ski technique. Nor is it a history of skiing. Nor, as the pictures on these two pages might indicate, is it a parody of skiing. Rather, it is intended as a panoramic view of the sport, with details on personalities, places, techniques, history—all the parts that have gradually come together to form the body and brain of American skiing. Throughout the book, there is an emphasis on pictures, because skiing is an excitingly visual sport. But the idea is to do more than provide something to look at. The idea is to tell a story, and the hope is that each picture, or sequence of pictures, or chapter of text, tells its own particular story. Not all the stories are complimentary: It is very hard to be anything but irritated by the silly politicking within the U. S. Ski Association, or by some of the pompous and basically dishonest attitudes

that drift like smog through high-level amateur racing. There is, however, very little ax grinding in this book. Most of the stories reflect the enthusiasm of one who has spent a fair portion of his professional life going skiing. It is a delightful sport, and the author has had a marvelous time at it—meeting people, skiing with them, finding new areas, new trails, new fashions, new equipment, new ways to ski. These pictures show that the author has not spent all his time looking graceful and triumphant. But whether he was struggling with a photographer's ladder under the unsympathetic eyes of Willy Schaeffler (below), or jackknifed helplessly in front of a young ski pupil, or losing a skirmish with a series of six-foot moguls at Arapahoe Basin, Colo., he has never ceased to enjoy the whole, happy business of being outdoors in winter on skis.

ACKNOWLEDGMENTS

Had it not been for some very skillful — and generous — people this book could never have been produced. Martin Nathan, Assistant Art Director for *Sports Illustrated,* gave much more of his time and energy in designing these pages than one could reasonably have asked for. I owe thanks, also, to Art Director Richard Gangel and the Picture Department for allowing the use of the magazine's facilities in the handling of photographs and photostats. Assistant Managing Editor Richard Johnston was kind enough to run a critical eye over the copy. My secretary, Elizabeth Waite, was very patient in handling many of the details. Peggy Downey and Janet Zich assisted in research, and Ted Stephney, Dorothy Merz, and Jean Lockhart of *Sports Illustrated*'s Picture Department solved many problems involving photographs and negatives. My special debt, however, is to the photographers. John Zimmerman took up skiing only five years ago; then, two years ago, he suddenly became the most imaginative ski photographer in the country. Perhaps I should not say "ski photographer," because Zimmerman is just as good in his approach to a dozen other sports. For purposes of this book, however, he is a ski photographer, and he has my ever-lasting thanks for the use of his pictures. Joern Gerdts stands beside Zimmerman in the ability to show skiing as the exciting and lovely sport that it is. When on an assignment Gerdts is nearly impossible to discourage or tire out. Another delightful thing about Gerdts is his method of coming downhill: He is the last skier in America to employ the pure style of Hannes Schneider, vintage 1932. Other photographers to whom I want to offer special thanks for major contributions are Margaret Durrance, Toni Frissell, Fred Lindholm, Jerry Cooke, Hanson Carroll, Ted Bronstein, and Franz Berko. There are, of course, many more photographers whose work appears in the book; to them, too, my thanks. And, finally, a word of gratitude to the private citizens such as Fritz Benedict, Otto Giese, Betty Woolsey, and my sister, Mrs. George Prince, who lent their time or their photographs.

CONTENTS

THE BOOK OF
AMERICAN SKIING

PART I

JUST ONCE LIKE STEIN

Skiers are divided into dreamers and wonderers. If they are young, they dream that someday they will ski like Stein Eriksen or Anderl Molterer, shown here as they swoop down the face of Ajax Mountain in Aspen, Colo., throwing plumes of snow, making each move with such assurance that they seem not to be standing on skis at all, but rather to be suspended from a wire. If the skier is a bit older, he will content himself with wondering how it feels to ski that way. At age 35, photographer John G. Zimmerman, who skis with great verve but modest skill, fits somewhere in between. To satisfy both impulses he rounded up Stein, Anderl, Toni Spiss and some other crack pros and went with them to some of the best mountains in the West. Each time one of the skiers headed down a slope, he would have a camera strapped to his leg or chest or back, tripping the shutter with a remote-control button as he hurtled along. The result is a dramatic portfolio of photographs that show dreamers and wonderers alike how it feels to ski a steep, deep mountain as well as it can be skied.

At left, Anderl Molterer's skis cut through the packed snow
as Stein Eriksen and Toni Spiss lead him off a jump at Alta,
Utah. Below, two Alta instructors play their own high-speed
game of follow-the-leader through a fall of hip-deep powder

The vast snowfields of the Continental Divide beneath their ski tips, Molterer and Olympic silver medalist Hans Peter Lanig (right) plunge off the edge of a trail along the northern rim of Arapahoe Basin, 12,000 feet up in the Colorado Rockies

Leaning into a turn, Toni Spiss (above) swings along behind Eriksen as they speed through the moguls on Aspen's lower slopes. At right, Molterer springs from a cornice and seems to float for an instant in the brilliant haze of the winter sun

As Molterer's speeding form almost disappears behind a spray of snow, Stein starts one of his swooping turns on the edge of the track just cut by Spiss's skis (foreground)

CHAPTER 1

WHERE IT BEGINS

No matter how spectacular Eriksen or Molterer or any of the rest of them may be now, at one time they looked very much like the young tiger at right, Herman Engler, staggering cheerfully down Dollar Mountain in Sun Valley. They may have been a bit older than Herman when they started, or they may have been younger. There really is no right or wrong age for a child to start skiing. Hannes Schneider, who systematized ski instruction first in Austria and later in America, used to say that eight or nine was the earliest anyone could be taught. But that was when ski equipment was so limp and soggy that it was a battle to learn even at eighteen. Austria's Olympic hero, Toni Sailer, says that below five, children cannot be taught — and this is probably true for formal instruction. But the best advice comes from someone infinitely less famous than the Austrian giants, though far better qualified on the subject of little children and snow. That is Glenn Springer-Miller, mother of two small objects and instructor of hundreds of others at the Sugar Bowl in California.

According to Mrs. Springer-Miller, "If they can walk, they can ski." That is, they can put on warm clothes, strap some short boards to their feet, and go out and have fun. This also permits their parents to put on warm clothes, strap on some longer boards, and go skiing, too, without having to spend a fortune on baby-sitters.

However, Mrs. Springer-Miller is very explicit on how long, and under what conditions, little kids should be put on skis. First of all, she says, they should have nothing less than the best gear. And best does not mean most expensive or most elaborate. Sturdy boots that fit are imperative. Single boots are fine — much more practical for youngsters than fancy double

boots, and good imported models cost only $15 or $20. Fit them over a single pair of heavy Norwegian natural wool socks. If you have to settle for Orlon or two pairs, be super-careful about wrinkles, which can raise blisters in half an hour.

continued

Glenn Springer-Miller tries to get through to one balky young pupil before the spirit of revolt spreads.

Skis now come ready-made with cable bindings, plastic bottoms (no waxing), and steel edges (essential for all ages). A young beginner's skis should be shorter than he is. Don't let an ignorant salesman sell him a pair that reach his lifted hand; the child's legs are too short to cope with skis measured by this ancient rule. Toe-iron bindings are fine for preschoolers; but when legs get longer and speed and leverage increase — say at about 8 — be sure they switch to release bindings.

Meanwhile, for the small fry, be absolutely certain the bindings are mounted with the toe of the boot behind the ski's halfway mark, even if this makes the tails look ridiculously short. Some manufacturers still put the binding platform too far forward, which makes learning to turn much harder. Total cost of skis and bindings: $20–25.

From the start, put the child in stretch pants (blue jeans soak up water like a kitchen sponge). Stretch pants are warmer, stay drier, the fabric is more durable, and, best of all, they grow with the child. Put long johns under the stretch pants. The fishnet type is best, but flannel pajamas do welcome double duty on a ski trip. Then, working north from the waist, add a fishnet top, a T shirt, one light and one heavy sweater, wool-lined leather mittens, goggles, and a knit cap. This wardrobe will be adequate for most days, but for the really bitter weeks in midwinter add a quilted parka. If this sounds like a lot of gear for one small skier, remember that many ski shops let you trade in outgrown equipment, and, if you have more than one child, everything can be handed down.

Once they have the right clothes and equipment, children will take to the slopes like snowshoe rabbits. They are natural skiers: flexible, with a low center of gravity, large impact area in a fall, short, thickly muscled legs, and plenty of subcutaneous fat. But bear in mind that children, like batteries, need frequent recharging in cold weather. When they seem tired, or complain of the cold, get them indoors right away. Put them in front of a fire and feed them hot drinks. A child has twice the skin area of an adult, relative to body weight or volume. Consequently his heat loss is enormous. He makes up for it, partly, with a higher metabolism; but this means, too, that when he is tired he is closer to exhaustion.

If you keep a close eye on him, he can start skiing before he is out of diapers. Once a two-year-old learns to get around, he finds that skis are much easier than feet in snow. Let him watch other children on skis. Let him walk around on the level. Don't start out with a long, dull explanation of the mechanics of a snowplow. Just let him play for a while. Give him

26

a cap pistol and let him play mountain troops; or start him in a game of tag, or follow-the-leader. He'll let you know when he's interested in trying the more complicated maneuvers.

When he asks you a question about how to ski, show him what to do by actually doing it. From the level take him up a slight incline. It doesn't matter whether you do a herringbone or a side step. He'll learn one or the other by imitation, by watching, by trying it himself. If you stand around talking, he may get cold. Certainly he'll get bored.

If he seems to be stuck, take his skis or boots gently in your hands and put them in the proper position for him. Hold his tips together in a snowplow while you ski backward. And if he tends to stick his weighty tail out behind to steer

with, like a little kangaroo, he's normal. If you resort to an occasional swat on it to remind him to keep it in, you're normal, too. All small children ski with their feet about two feet apart, their arms held out wide for balance. Don't interfere with this position; he'll straighten up when his waist gets farther from the ground.

When he wants to ride the tow, let him, but go up with him. Put his skis between yours and be prepared to hold him up at any point. A small child can get tangled up in amazing ways. *Absolutely no poles* or loose clothing for either of you on a rope tow. The more he skis without poles, the better his balance will be, anyway. And, above all, don't push him into anything he doesn't really want to try. After all, skiing is for fun, and there really is no other point, is there?

27

Fun and Games to Keep Them Going

After a young skier has had a little time to flounder around and get used to the snow, he is ready to join other kids in a real ski class. In these early classes, he should be introduced *slowly* to the techniques of skiing. Even though the age group for formal instruction is higher (6–11) than that discussed by Glenn Springer-Miller, some of her rules should still be followed: Don't let the youngsters get cold; don't push them too fast (their natural tendency to show

Schaeffler shows basic walking step, taking gliding strides, using the poles with natural rhythm of arm swing.

off will have them pushing you, anyway), and don't launch into any long drawn-out speeches about how they should be doing things. Notice that below and on the following pages, the ski teacher is doing everything with the children, not lining them up like an infantry platoon while the wind howls around them. This is something for instructors of pupils of all ages to remember. There is nothing that stiffens a beginner, six or sixty, faster than standing in a cold wind, or in a coldly formal class. The instructor shown here is Willy Schaeffler, director of the 1960 Olympic ski events and coach of the national champion Denver University ski team. He is also director of the Rocky Mountain News Free Ski School; as such, each year he takes on 1800 beginners of all ages. These are some of the exercises he gives them. Each one has in it some movement that will be useful later on. And each one, if it is properly taught, also can be fun to learn.

In game of follow-the-leader, Schaeffler starts on short tour (above) moving from level to gently rolling ground. Then he leads his pupils in skating on skis, a slow, easy exercise that is much like ice skating and gives youngsters a sense of balance.

Photographs by Margaret Durrance

Ski poles set up alternately as low bridge (background) and tight squeeze teach up-and-down movements of the knees and ankles that skiers will need later when they first go onto bumpy terrain.

Tossing up poles and trying to catch them at start of first little downhill run — or leaving mitten to be scooped up from snow (right) — gets youngsters' *minds off their skis. This is a vital exercise, since major sin of nearly all beginners and intermediates is to stare at their skis rather than at the terrain ahead.*

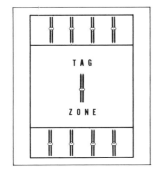 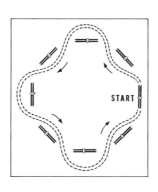 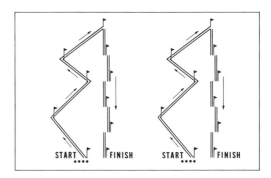

Here are a few informal games to make the learning process more fun. At left is a sort of tag game. Everybody gets rid of his poles; then, the one who is "it" stands in no-man's land — the tag zone. The others line up in safety zones in front of him and behind. The "it" man gives the word to start, then tries to tag the others as they dash back and forth between the safety zones. Last man caught is "it" for the next round. This game should be played on fairly flat ground, and is the best thing in the world for getting children or adults over any feeling of awkwardness about being on skis. Another good game is the square dance (center), in which one pupil weaves in and out through a circle of others, learning to change direction as he goes. Relay race (right), with side step and zigzag, teaches balance and direction change. Anyone who tries to force the side step or the sharp turns in the zigzag will wind up in the snow. Anyone who makes it is ready to go up the practice hill.

31

The first time a skier starts down a steep slope (left), he probably will be scared. Pick a short slope, and let him start across it, stepping up into slope if he gets going too fast.

Herringbone is fastest way to walk uphill. Difficult for adults because of the long tails on grown-up skis, herringbone is easy for youngsters whose short skis do not tend to cross each other in back.

Kick turn is tricky for novices, but useful for everyone. Show pupil how, then let him try it. Make sure he plants poles out from skis, and tell him to kick hard so tail of ski does not catch in snow.

When the youngster is ready to go straight down, tell him to drop his poles. Then, as he starts, have him touch boots. This gets weight forward, and keeps skis from running away.

As confidence grows, teach kids a few tricks — but make them helpful tricks. This one is good for balance, and gives feeling of riding on a single ski, as in advanced parallel skiing.

Once the class has gotten some confidence, and its members begin to handle their skis naturally, they are ready for the big hill. Here Schaeffler shows basic running position: skis together, knees and hips bent, uphill shoulder forward, arms relaxed.

IF THEY WANT, LET THEM TRY

If a kid learns quickly, and really loves skiing, there is no reason why, one day, he should not be allowed to race. Most resorts — and some public schools in the West — have good junior programs. Unfortunately, quite a few parents are against letting children compete on the grounds that someone may get hurt; or — horrors — that a child might want to win too much. Well, maybe he will want to win; if he's good enough, let him. If he's not, the other kids will teach him how to lose a lot better than a parent who won't allow him to compete at all. As for getting hurt, he is in just as much danger when riding a bike or climbing a tree, two pastimes this nation seems to have survived. But don't force any child into racing. A boy like Jimmy Huega, shown above at age 11, will take to it naturally and prosper at it. Today, at 20, Jimmy is an international racer who has traveled, competed, won, lost, and grown a lot through skiing. Most kids will never be as good as Jimmy, but they can have just as much fun winning and losing in local ski races.

CHAPTER 2

THE MURKY PAST

Anyone who starts taking ski lessons these days has to endure an awful load of theory on how to ski, and a fair number of arguments about who really started what. There are two defenses against this situation: one is to ignore it; the other is to learn a little something. On the assumption that the people who bought this book are at least curious about skiing, the next few pages contain a brief chronology of who did what that mattered.

About 3000 years before Christ, Norse hunters started mushing after animals and each other with the aid of primitive skis. Until the 18th century A.D., one wooden ski of a pair tended to be a good deal longer than the other; the long one was the running platform, and the short one was a sort of rudder. With this arrangement, the hunter or soldier was able to slide along fairly well on level ground, and even to charge downhill — assuming he did not care what obstacles were at the bottom. Nobody had the vaguest idea of how to turn, much less come to a standing stop, from speeds above three miles an hour.

Then, for better or worse, came the first glimmerings of technique. A long pole was dragged behind to help the skier keep his balance, to slow down and, finally, to turn. Up to this point skiing was strictly a Norse phenomenon, and more a means of transportation than a sport, although, as we shall see, there were a few informal races here and there. Then, in the middle of the 19th century, skiing leaped all the way to California without first touching down in Central Europe. It was brought to California by Scandinavian miners who went into the Sierra looking for gold. And by this time it had become a sport. On pages 230–233 of this book there are photographs of a crew of forty-niners in a race (they competed for money in those days — a practice which, in the past two years, has been brought back into the open).

The most renowned skier of that time, and the first American skier of any consequence, was a mail carrier and sometime racer named Snowshoe Thomson, shown here in the heroic yet somewhat startled attitude of 19th-century sports figures. Thomson flourished from 1856 to 1876, carrying letters, and anything else he could cram into his rucksack (capacity: 100 lbs.) 90 miles over the Sierra from Genoa to Hangtown. He achieved all this on the monstrous 12-foot skis of the day, held by toe straps and heel-block bindings. His only defense against onrushing trees was the single-pole drag system; for turning, a firm backward and sideward lean; for stopping, lean way back and hope for the best. Awkward and ineffective as it was, the pole-drag gambit died a slow death: as late as 1929 Elon Jessup was advocating it in his technique book, *Skis and Ski-ing* (E. P. Dutton & Co.).

That, for all practical purposes, is the ancient history of skiing. If you are a Norwegian, it is satisfying to know that the first skis seen in the Alps were brought there in 1883 by a Norwegian expedition to the Monastery of St. Bernard. If you are an Austrian, it is comforting to think that an Austrian inventor named Mathias Zdarsky was the first great promoter of skiing as an Alpine sport, circa 1900. And if you are English, you can ponder with pride the fact that when Sir Henry Lunn persuaded some of his British friends to spend a few winter days in Chamonix, France, in 1898, he started the entire business of winter-sport tourism. But if, like the author, you are simply an American who likes to ski, then turn the page to see the men and the movements that transformed this chaos into a delightful and not too difficult sport.

FIRST REAL TURN

Some time before Snowshoe Thomson and his forty-niner friends made their monumental appearance in California, a group of Norwegian farmers in the county of Telemark began skiing strictly for fun. At first they made do with the pole drag. Then some courageous and impatient man, tired of dragging either his pole or his backside, decided that what skiing needed was a real turn. Whereupon he thrust one ski forward until its binding was even with the tip of the other ski; then he edged the leading ski in the direction he wanted to go, put his weight on it, and leaned backward and in toward the direction of the turn. Thus was born the telemark, the first true turn. Up to World War I, the telemark was *the* turn, used by the early racers such as Marius Eriksen (right), who was famous first as a ski champion (1905-15), and much later as the father of the formidable Stein.

WORST REAL TURN

The successor to the telemark was a disaster called the scissor christie — also known as the open christie, steered christie, or *scheren* christie. This mildly suicidal means of changing direction flourished from World War I until roughly the mid-Twenties. Like the telemark, it owes its name to a locale in Norway, in this case the tiny village of Christiania, which has ever since been held responsible for about half of the dozen different kinds of turns that skiers have used. The christie at left is demonstrated by Luggi Foegger, one of the first Austrian skiers to come to the U. S. To make a scissor, the skier starts downhill; then he takes all the weight off one ski, edges that ski outward, and lets the tip drift outward. When the drift is well established, he shifts his weight to the drifting ski, and leans back and into the turn. If the gods happen to be smiling that day, there will truly be a wide-radius turn. If not, each ski will seek its swift and separate way.

A PROPHET NAMED HANNES

In the midst of this babble of voices, there appeared a tall, hawk-faced Austrian from the Arlberg region named Hannes Schneider. Hannes was born June 24, 1890, in the tiny village of Stuben, where a pioneer skier named Viktor Sohm showed him a new kind of turn called the stem. This was a safe and simple maneuver, in which the heel of one ski was thrust outward until the ski was pointing in the direction the skier wanted to go. Then the weight was transferred to that ski, and around he went. Starting with this turn, adding the snowplow — a rudimentary brake accomplished by pushing the tails of the skis outward — and developing them through his early career as a ski instructor for mountain troops in World War I, Schneider changed the whole concept of ski technique. And in so doing, he systematized the sport so it could be easily taught.

Schneider brought the skier down low, where he could work with his skis. Knees and hips were bent, and the shoulders brought forward so the skier looked like a man sitting in a chair, leaning forward to hear better. Schneider's basic turn was built on the snowplow, and the half snowplow or stem. In a turn to the left the tail of the ski was pushed out first, as a kind of speed check and body windup. At the same time, the skier crouched even lower, cranked back his right shoulder, and started stemming the right ski. Then he straightened up, unwound and, as the skis swung around through the turn, sank back into his crouch again. This turn, its variations and the position from which they started, was called the Arlberg system of skiing. It was taught all over Europe in the late 1920's and throughout the 1930's. Hannes himself brought it to North America when he moved permanently to North Conway, N. H., in 1939 following the *Anschluss*.

THE FRENCH OCCUPATION

For a time, Arlberg skiing was the True Word and Hannes Schneider was its prophet. Then, at the 1936 Winter Olympics in Garmisch, a ski pro named Anton Seelos went off as forerunner for the slalom. Keeping his skis parallel all the way, and making his turns with shoulder rotation alone, he finished five seconds ahead of the official winner, a stem-turning amateur. Suddenly parallel skiing was the rage. Though Seelos first made it fashionable, the one to make capital of parallel skiing was a handsome Frenchman named Emile Allais. Allais declared a moratorium on the snow-plow and stem. Now, all a beginner needed to know was the sideslip. From there, with a shoulder windup, a forward-leaning swoop, and perhaps a heel-kicking *ruade* (left) for an added flourish — *voilà,* the skier was making parallel turns. Alas, the miracle came true only for Allais and his confreres on the French team, which dominated ski racing in the 1940's. For the real secret of the French system was not so much in the method of skiing as in the wonderfully acrobatic bodies of its skiers. Thus, by about 1950, the *Méthode Allais* died of Emile & Co.'s aging reflexes.

THE TRUE FAITH RESTORED

During the brief rule of Allais, there was no joy in Austria. The national pride could hardly stand the loss of its leadership in skiing. The national pocketbook was in much the same condition. Ski victories equals ski tourists, and with Marshall Plan dollars putting up lifts, ski tourism was becoming Austria's number-two industry. It was with rapture that the nation hailed four new heroes: Franz Gabl, Eddi Mall, Hans Nogler, and Christian Pravda. Using a more upright and ultimately more parallel version of the old Arlberg technique, these four began beating the French team, thus bringing both the standard of skiing — and the dollars — back home. Among those who shared Austria's happiness were Friedl Pfeifer, discoverer of the ski potential of Aspen, Colo., and Fred Iselin (right), who now heads Aspen's Buttermilk ski school. They had made good money teaching the modern Arlberg system to American pupils. Now the top racers had canonized this method; Arlberg was ascendant again.

40

BUT THEN — A NEW HERESY

No sooner had Austria begun winning again than some of her racers started using a new technique. At first no one was quite sure what it was. All they knew was that when a good racer ran a tight slalom, he went through the gates without rotating his shoulders in the direction of his turns. Instead he seemed to slither down the course, fishtailing his skis through the turns with a quick swing of the hips. The racers nicknamed it *wedeln,* Tyrolean slang for "tail-wagging." A few Swiss observers called it the old *gegenschulter,* a kind of hopping, shoulder-shrugging means of making a turn without rotating the upper body. Some Austrians called it "delayed shoulder," and said that the feet and skis moved so fast that the shoulders lagged farther and farther behind until, quite by accident, they turned in the opposite direction from the skis. But high on a mountain above St. Christoph, a tight little group of physical education specialists, among them a supple Kitzbühler named Franz Furtner (above), were finding out what was really happening to both the shoulders and the skis. To see what they discovered and how these discoveries changed skiing, turn page.

CHAPTER 3

THE SHORTSWING

Kruckenhauser discovered the shortswing in Austria.

Willy Schaeffler spread the word to skiers in America.

Franz Furtner was one of several dozen men — among them a hatful of Olympic medal winners — who had been invited to St. Christoph to ski and talk and observe until they found out how the modern racers made their hip-swiveling turns. The overseer of the project was Stefan Kruckenhauser, Professor of Biology and Sport at the University of Innsbruck and absolute ruler over the system of training, examining, and certifying Austrian ski teachers. Kruckenhauser himself skied with all the delicate grace of a polar bear. But he had plenty of skiing virtuosos in his stable. His own contributions were an analytical brain, a stubborn will, and a battery of cameras.

Like all good researchers, Kruckenhauser and Co. started by sifting old knowledge. They went back to Hannes Schneider and beyond, until they arrived at the original stem turn. They picked it up, turned it over, took it apart, and eventually saw that the moving force in a stem turn was not shoulder rotation, or the down – UP – down motion, but simply a change of weight from one ski to the other.

With this much in hand, they pushed on to 1928, the year an engineer named Rudolph Lettner patented the first set of steel edges; and they noted that at about the same time bindings were getting tighter. These two developments in equipment gave the skier much better control, and let him straighten up from his deep Arlberg crouch. The trail then led straight to Toni Seelos, with his parallel rotation turns — which obviously were faster and more elegant than any stem — and to Emile Allais, with his sideslipping, skis-together *Méthode Française*.

All through his historical analysis, Kruckenhauser could see that the more upright a man stood, and the more relaxed he was, and the more he kept his skis together, the less effort he needed to make his turns. This brought the hunters abreast of the modern Arlbergers, who had become so quick in their turns that sometimes their

In old-fashioned Arlberg stem turn (right), skier first made a downhill stem, wound up his shoulders, then swung around with a down-up-down motion of knees and hips. In the shortswing, he stems his uphill ski, shifts his weight, and swings through the turn with a minimum of effort.

shoulders seemed to lag behind their skis. From here it was only a half step to *wedeln,* and the original mystery of why a *wedeler wedeled.*

After another agony of analysis, abetted by thousands of feet of film of all the best *wedelers* on all types of slopes and snow, Kruckenhauser came to the conclusion that changed ski technique all over the world. The new-style turns were made by thrusting the heels in one direction while the shoulders actually turned in the opposite direction as a counterforce for the heel thrust. This reverse shoulder movement was a true revolution in skiing, not just a racer's idiosyncrasy. As for the hips, they acted as a swivel between the opposite movements of shoulders and feet. The waggling motion the racers called *wedeln* was a result of the fluid, side-to-side movement of the feet and legs.

Having discovered this powerful new medicine, Kruckenhauser decided to swallow it whole. Reverse shoulder was the best way to ski. Now the problem was to find out how to start with a beginner and take him through a series of simple, logical steps until he could make heel-thrusting parallel turns.

To set up his teaching sequence, Kruckenhauser made one more dive into history, scooped up what he needed, and then surfaced to put it all together in the simple, graceful, functional system of skiing called the "shortswing."

From the French he took the notion that all skiing should begin with a traverse and a sideslip. This made good sense on the bumpy, hardpacked snow at modern resorts, where a skier spends half his time traversing or sideslipping to get to the best place to turn. Furthermore, the

continued

In comma position, feet and knees are together, weight is on downhill ski. Knees and backside are angled toward the mountain, hips and shoulders face downhill. Upper body is out over the skis.

edge control he learns from sideslipping is the same edge control he uses to carve his turns later on.

Since it was impossible to start a well-controlled sideslip — and ultimately a heel-thrust turn — from the old, straight-ahead traverse position, Kruckenhauser devised a new position (above) called the "comma." From it, a skier can easily start a heel thrust, a slideslip, or continue traversing, as he chooses.

Next, said Kruckenhauser, the pupil would learn a parallel swing to the slope, which is little more than a traverse with a gentle heel push tossed in. At this point, the new system departed from the French pattern, with its quick leap to parallel skiing, and went back instead to Schneider for the snowplow to give the novice some way of holding down his speed the first time he headed down the mountain. Next came a snowplow turn. Then a stem turn; then the more advanced stem swing (a stem turn that ends with a heel push); then the single parallel turn. And finally, for the real experts, the quick, linked turns that had been the original cause of the entire upheaval. Every one of these maneuvers, from the snowplow turn to the so-called *wedeln,* was started with a weight shift and finished with a heel thrust, with a reflection of the comma at the start and finish of each turn.

With the system worked out, Kruckenhauser pronounced it law for all ski instructors in Austria. That was in 1953. Then he lined up a team of crack demonstrators, the best of whom was Franz Furtner, and at the International Ski Instructor's Congress in 1955, showed the world what was new in Austria. Some of the world didn't care. Switzerland never cares what anyone else does. In France, a few people cared, but they were too hung over from their indulgence in Allais to do much about it.

In America, there were only three people who really cared. One was Karl Hinderman in Big Mountain, Mont., but his ski school was at that time too small and out of the way to make much difference. Another was Paul Valar, of Franconia, N. H., who had plenty of pupils. But they were the conservative, snowplowing Boston kind, not prone to grab a new thing and travel around spreading the good word. One other person who cared was Willy Schaeffler, and Willy happened to be the right man in the right place for American skiing. His Denver University ski team was on the crest of an unprecedented streak of national championships; his Rocky Mountain News Free Ski School was flourishing, and, in the fall of 1957, *Sports Illustrated* asked him to do a series of articles on the new skiing technique.

The articles got a reception that could best be described as loud, since there were some hearty boos mixed with the other sounds. A lot of old skiers thought the whole thing was nonsense. Some others thought it looked pretty good, but they would have too much trouble changing over.

At Aspen, a fortress of rotation, the day the first article came out, Iselin and co-director Friedl Pfeifer called a hasty meeting of their ski school and, according to one of the instructors, told everyone that no matter what they might read in *Sports Illustrated,* they were to keep rotating.

No matter who was ruffled by the shortswing, most skiers in the U. S. started to use it, with pleasure and with fairly good success. Since then, the technique has been modified, and for the better. The reverse shoulder has become less pronounced; there is more emphasis on knee action; and the snowplow has resumed its rightful place at the head of the teaching line, mostly because the average skier is not about to spend three days practising a traverse in the comma position before he tries to make his first turn. However, the basic teachings of Kruckenhauser are still there, and they will be around for a long time to come.

Drawings by Robert Riger

Top and front view of shortswinger show that hips, shoulders always face downhill. Upper body is erect, but knees and ankles are pressed forward to keep tails of skis free to swing and body at proper angle.

Just Do Them

While the idea of skiing may be lovely, the idea of getting in shape to ski is pretty dreary, especially in the early morning, which is the only time most people can spare for exercise. There will be no claims here that the exercises on these pages are fun. They aren't. All exercises are a bore. So the thing to do is not to think about them; just do them. Start on October 1, and go for 10 minutes every weekday until the season starts. Then cut to Tuesdays and Thursdays. If, by April, the old frame is still looking a bit soggy, you might keep working out all year. Women especially will find these exercises great year-round streamliners.

In change-step jump, start with right foot in front of left, right shoulder advanced, body bent left in reflection of comma. Then jump up, switching position of feet, reversing shoulders before landing. Start with 10 times right and left; add one a day up to 20.

Buddha squat toughens stomach muscles, stretches and loosens thighs. Start in the position shown; roll down on one shoulder and keep going until you are on your back. Then roll back up. If you don't make it, keep fighting. Once is enough to start.

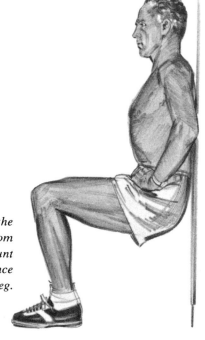

Phantom chair is best exercise for the thighs and the knees. Stand with back to wall, feet 18 inches from base of wall. Sink to sitting position, hold for count (slow and honest) of 15. Then rest and do it once more. When you can hold it for 30, try one leg.

Stooper's strut is agony for men but easy for women. This exercise is, however, vital for both sexes, since it stretches and toughens Achilles tendon, a vulnerable sinew in middle-aged skiers. Touch toes, keep knees straight. Men start with 10, women 20.

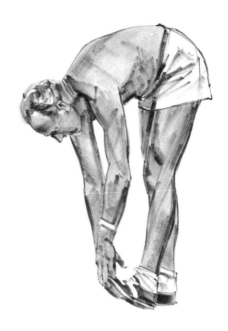

Split jump is least ingenious of exercises but best for wind; it is also good for thighs, feet, and ankles. Stand with feet together, jump up and do fore and aft split. Land on your toes and jump again, switching leg and arm position in air. Ten times at first.

Front split stretches everything, including patience, but it is last exercise, so let's get it done. Lie on stomach; do push-up and hold arms stiff. Throw feet forward and out so they land on line with hands. Jump back to prone position. Five times.

CHAPTER 4   KNEEMANSHIP

And now class, we are going on the mountain. Before we do, remember these four things: (1) Be loose and easy. Skiing is a dance, not a wrestling match, and no one has yet managed to outmuscle a mountain. (2) Keep your eyes and weight forward. You are going downhill, so look where you are going; and keep your body moving downhill, out with the skis, not back. (3) Use your knees. *Skilaufen ist Knielaufen* (old Ger. prov.): skiing is kneeing (Eng. trans.). Your knees give balance, spring, and power. Bend them — and the ankles — forward, so you feel pressure on the fronts of your boots. (4) Stop skiing when you are tired. Ski doctors would starve if everybody skipped the last run of the day.

Photographs by John G. Zimmerman

THE SNOWPLOW

The snowplow is a brake, and it is also the beginning of edge control. Push the tails of your skis out, but keep the tips almost touching; flex your knees forward and in. Feel the gentle forward pressure on the fronts of your boots; do not sit back and do not strain. To start moving, shift the knees slightly outward. To stop, bring them back in. Do everything lightly. Your skis should brush over the snow, not dig in. To make a snowplow turn (right), get moving in the plow position. To turn right, bend upper body sideways to the left, and bend left knee forward and in. To go the other way, shift upper body to right, and bend right knee. The weight shift starts the turn, the knee bend concentrates the weight forward and on the inside edge so the tail of the ski can swing through the arc of the turn.

48

THE SIDESLIP

Once you bring your feet and knees together, as you must for good skiing, life seems more precarious. The broad, tricycle stability of the snowplow is gone. Now you have to learn to handle your edges, as you started to do in the snowplow, and as you *must* do from now on. A sideslip is carried out from the comma position, i.e., the basic traverse position. And it is controlled with the knees, not with the ankles as is so often taught. In fact, if your weight is forward as it should be when skiing, you cannot roll your ankles at all; they are locked and will not turn. Your knees, however, are free to do the work.

In the sideslip, as in all other phases of skiing, your weight should be on the downhill ski; and it is the action of the downhill knee that decides what happens to your skis. Stand with your skis pointing across the slope and the downhill knee just inside the centerline of the boot. To start sideslipping, shift your downhill knee outward; the edges of your skis will loosen their grip on the snow and will start to slip. Keep your body out over the skis; if you lean in toward the mountain, you will shortly be lying in the snow. To stop slipping, make a fairly sharp inward movement of the knees with a strong weight emphasis on the downhill leg; the edges of the skis will bite into the snow and you will stop.

50

SWING
TO THE SLOPE

This is your first parallel turn, but it is really no more than a graduate version of the sideslip. Instead of aiming your skis across the slope, you head diagonally down the mountain; and instead of sliding sideways, you make an easy, heel-brushing turn in toward the hill. However, the running position is the same as the sideslip, and the movements are very similar. Get going at a slow, comfortable speed with skis and knees together, weight on the outside ski, hips and shoulders turned downhill in the comma position (top right). Then, while leaning the upper body slightly forward from the ankles, flex the outside knee and draw it in toward the slope. The forward shifting of weight makes the forward edges of the skis bite in, while the tails of the skis become free to swing through the turn. As the skis start to swing, swivel your shoulders gently in the opposite direction from the turn. You will now be moving through the arc on the turn, and your body will be coiled like a spring, ready to make the heel thrust that ends all shortswing turns. Here again the knee action controls the maneuver. If you edge the skis sharply and thrust hard as shown at right below, you will stop dead. If you use less knee action, edging more subtly and making a gentler thrust, you will slow momentarily and then continue your descent. Whatever you do will be done primarily with the knees, just as it was in the side-slip, the only differences being the slight forward weight shift and the easy reverse shoulder movement. Practice this turn over and over again without looking at your skis, and be sure that your upper body stays out over the skis, never tipping backward or in toward the mountain.

THE STEM TURN

About 90 per cent of all skiers use the stem turn, with varying degrees of polish. As soon as the novice begins to get his feet together, his snowplow turn quickly works into a stem. And it usually stays there forever. The experts use it, too. If you were to watch slow-motion movies of the world's flashiest parallel skiers, you would see that when they are tired, or careless, or in momentary doubt, they will use a tiny stem. The turn itself, shown here on a gentle, packed slope, combines all the elements discussed on the preceding four pages. Start off in the comma, with knees and skis together, weight on the downhill ski as in the side-slip, and swing to the slope. Then, stem out with the uphill ski, and bend the knee of the uphill ski in and down as you shift the weight onto that ski. As you come through the fall line – the line of steepest descent down the hill – keep the knee of the weighted ski forward so the tails will be free to swing, and keep that same knee just inside the track of the ski so your inside edge will be carving the turn just as it did in the snowplow. Once past the fall line, bring the inside ski back alongside the outside ski and come to a stop with a gentle heel push. When you can make one fairly good turn, then link two turns together, one in each direction. Then do a series. As you practice, keep making the angle of the stem narrower and narrower. Start the heel push earlier, and make it a longer, stronger movement. You are now doing the stem swing, a graceful, functional turn beyond which the week-end skier need not go for a safe, satisfactory trip down any mountain.

THE PARALLEL TURN

There is too much emphasis these days on parallel technique. The only reason to ski is to have fun, and if fun for you is stem-swinging down someone's mountain, then enjoy it, and don't let anybody tell you that you're not skiing. However, if fun for you is doing something really well, then try the parallel turn. Until now, nothing has been said about the poles, because you haven't needed them, except for an occasional forward push or maybe to lean on when you were getting up. But now that the stem is being abandoned, you are going to use your poles to help get the turn started. Start off in a fairly steep traverse, weight on the downhill ski, upper ski ahead. At the point when you would have started stemming, press forward and slightly down with the knees. Then, with a very soft springing motion, come up and forward. The instant you start up, touch — do not jam — the inside pole to the snow, shift your weight to the outside ski, and turn your shoulders smoothly in the opposite direction from the turn. As you come through for the finishing heel push, be sure the downhill knee is forward and in toward the slope, the upper body is out over the skis. Also be sure, as you come through the fall line, to move the inside ski ahead to keep the tips from crossing. Finally, remember not to plant the pole until you start up, and do not lean on it as you go around. All turns are made with weight shift and heel thrust; the pole is a minor aid for providing lift and proper timing.

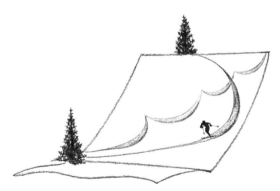

If you have trouble with your first parallel turns — and you will — try making a swing to the slope. Then make another and another, each time starting more sharply downhill and swinging up more sharply. Then take the plunge through the fall line.

55

WEDELN

This is the ultimate in shortswing skiing on a packed slope, a series of quick parallel turns, with the heel thrust at the end of one turn providing the lift to start the next one. The demonstrator here, as on the previous pages, is Dr. Clemens Hutter, who studied under Kruckenhauser at his skiing laboratory at St. Christoph. Like all the best shortswingers, however, Hutter has modified his movements since he first learned the technique. The exaggerated reverse shoulder is gone. The upper body is quiet, the shoulders providing only a slight reverse as they keep facing down the mountain while the skis slither back and forth. Even the hips show very little motion. The important action is in the knees — side to side, down and forward, with a subtle pole touch for each turn.

Survival Among
the Moguls

When a slope has been skied a lot, and people have turned in the same places all day, big mounds of snow called moguls begin to sprout. Sometimes the moguls are only a few inches high, and sometimes, like the ones shown here at Arapahoe Basin, Colo., they are six feet high, with deep ruts between them. This takes some skiing. You have to be quick; your weight has to be forward; before you even reach the fall line in one turn you must prepare (second figure from top) for the next one; you will need all the knee action you can muster; and you must finish each turn with a powerful heel thrust. If you skip one of these essentials, you will either fall backward or gain five mph at each mogul — in the latter case your speed after eight moguls will be quite impressive. In the sequence below, Olympic medalist Hans Peter Lanig does everything right. He stays close to the fall line, but never goes faster than 10 to 15 mph. For the key to his performance, turn the page.

START EVERY TURN WITH A HEEL THRUST

When a skier like Lanig comes through a steep field of moguls, the key to his control is the heel thrust. His action is the same as that used by Hutter on a smooth, gentle slope, but the movements are stronger. As a help in setting up the turns, a lot of good skiers use a quick heel thrust to start the first turn. Moving across the slope

in his initial traverse (1), the skier comes forward with his knees and prepares to plant his pole (2). Then he makes a quick downhill thrust with his heels (3), making sure the weight is on the downhill ski and the upper body is out over the skis. At the end of the heel thrust, he stops the skis from swinging by digging the uphill edges into the snow. The instant after they stop, he plants the pole and swings the tail of his skis back uphill (4), blending the end of the heel thrust into the beginning of the uphill move-

ment. Then he swings through the fall line (5) and again comes forward and down with the knees (6) to end the turn. Figures A, B, and C below correspond to 2, 3, and 4 at left, and are the heart of the turn. Notice that there is a slight reverse movement of the shoulder as the heel thrust starts. Don't overdo this reverse. It is a very subtle countermovement, not a powerful wrench that might throw your body weight back onto the uphill ski. Remember that most of the work is done by the skis and legs; the upper body should make no more commotion than is necessary to counterbalance the heel thrust and plant the pole. As you can see from A, B, and C, this is hardly any commotion at all. Finally, use all the heel thrust you need to check your speed and provide a platform to start the next turn. Be strong and quick, but don't be violent. This is expert stuff, and you're going to spend some time reclining on the snow before you master it. But when you finally do, you'll be as good a trail skier as a nonracer ever needs to be.

B

A

Lean Back a Bit in Powder

After being snarled at for three or four years to get his weight forward when skiing a packed slope, the average man will be comforted by Rule No. 1 for skiing deep powder: get the weight back. This is the canon of all good powder-snow skiers, the best of whom is Junior Bounous (right), head of the ski school at the Sugar Bowl in California. Get in your regular downhill position with weight (white dot at left) concentrated just behind the ski tips. Then, hold knee and hip position, and come back a bit from ankles. Your weight will now be over your boots, and you will have the feeling of sitting lightly on a high chair. Why do this? See below.

On a packed slope, your skis move fast, and you keep your weight out where the skis are going. Also, when you are skiing on a firm surface, there is no problem about the tips diving. Furthermore, because of the firm surface you can use a stiff ski whose edges will take a strong grip on the snow.

In deep powder, there is more snow resistance and your skis move more slowly. The problem is not so much to keep up with your skis as to get your skis up on top of the snow where they can work. If your weight is too far forward, the tips will dive and you will dive after them. Therefore, bring your weight back to the boots; this helps bring the tips up. Another help is to use softer skis that tend to rise up even when the weight is too far forward.

The other rules for powder are: use plenty of knee lift as Bounous is doing to get the skis swinging; look for steep slopes where extra speed helps you get through your turns; and avoid panic — a deep snow turn is easy, but not if you bail out halfway through.

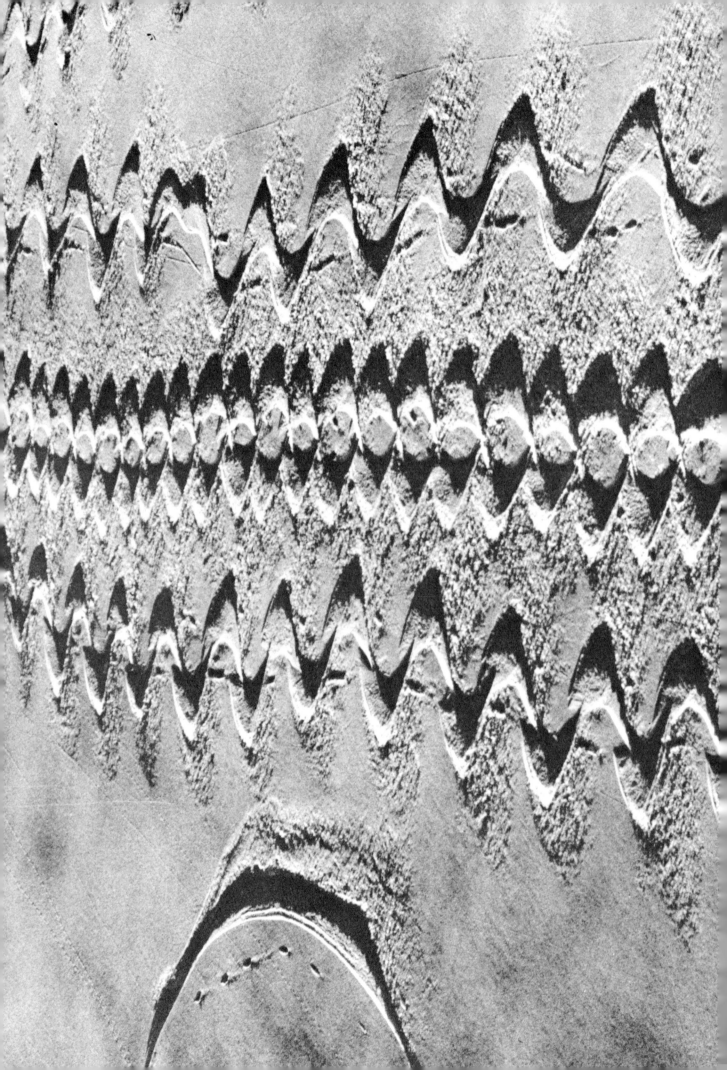

Photograph by Stefan Kruckenhauser

WHICH BRINGS US BACK
TO STEIN AND THE BOYS

If you were a marvelous athlete, and skied every day for 15 years, you could make tracks like those above, carved in an Austrian snowfield. You're not and you can't (probably), but there is no harm in dreaming. Once or twice a season you just might do everything right, and make two or three — or even 10 or 12 — good turns. The rest of the time, well, the fire is just as warm and the rum just as good after a series of stout stem turns.

CHAPTER 5

VOICES OF DISSENT

What you have read about ski technique on the preceding pages is the gospel according to St. Christoph. However, there are other books in the skiers' bible, one of which was written by Fred Iselin, an ordained Arlberger. At the mention of the phrase "reverse shoulder," Fred goes into spasms of protest, which are both good-humored and well-informed. Here is a recent sermon, delivered to a doubter (the author) in Aspen:

Iselin runs Buttermilk ski school in Aspen, Colo.

What we need is more normalcy in skiing. With that reverse shoulder, how can I do that from 8:30 in the morning until six at night? Poking along, picking along. Maybe if I am in the moguls and I am standing up to see where I am going, and I make some fast turns, maybe then my shoulders get behind my skis and I look like I am skiing with the reversed shoulder. Or if I am running a slalom and I must make two-three-four tight gates in a hurry and I start out with rotation pretty soon my shoulder gets behind. Or if I am in the slalom, and being a rough guy and leading with my shoulder like this because I may bang into the pole, then I am for a moment in reverse. But if I start out that way, in the reverse, then I am already behind my skis, and after I go through a tight flush my skis are way ahead of me and I am not on them any more and I fall.

"Those short skis. Have you tried them? Those little things — it is like walking to the post office. They chatter with me when I am sitting on the lift. You say they are good for the fifty-five-year-old doctor who is taking up skiing? Look, when I play tennis do I come out on the court with a racquet ten feet square and say 'I'm

fifty-five years old?' No. It is not tennis. Before that I give up the sport.

"Look, with your own skis there, I think they are too short. How long are they? Seven foot? Two ten? I think you need two fifteen. You do better with a longer ski. There is only one way to measure a ski. I think you ran a thing in your magazine there — I know it was Friedl that said it. He said you measure a ski by the weight of the skier. I took that to him, and I said 'Friedl, look, we got one skier here who is five feet ten and a half and he weighs three hundred ten pounds. How long are his skis? Sixteen feet?' No. It is ridiculous.

"There is only one way to measure the ski. That is, you reach up straight with the arm and bend the hand over and that is how long the ski should be. You, with the two ten would do better with a longer ski. They will track better, and in the soft snow they will not dive the way you say those ones will. And your poles I think could be two inches shorter. What are they — fifty-eight? I think fifty-six is better. The slalom racers are using the shorter poles, so when they are forward and reaching, it is smooth, and the poles do not jerk them up. And on the trail they are just as easy to turn, just as easy.

"Now my main idea is I must be with my skis. With my skis. Where are my skis taking me? And that is where I must be. Out here, out, forward. Not back here all cramped up in that reverse shoulder position. I mean, how unnatural can I get? How unnatural can I be? I am turning one way, my skis are turning one way and my shoulders are turning the other. I am sitting way back, which is wrong, and it makes me lean into the mountain, which is wrong. No. I must be with my skis.

"And if I am skiing, just skiing to have fun, how can I poke along like that all day. Where is the joy of skiing? The lightness, the floating, that is the real joy. How can I make those long turns that are so much fun if I am all twisted around in that unnatural position? You must have that lightness, that rhythm, that floating like a dancer. We have some pupils here that are dancers, like Dan Dailey, Gene Kelly. He is not a pupil here now, but those dancers can go from the snowplow right up to parallel skiing in almost a day and a half. They have the rhythm, the lightness. That is the secret. I must not be down pushing the snow with my heels, shoving. I must be up, skiing gracefully, light.

"Besides, those good skiers, when they get going fast, when they get in trouble, or they are in that difficult snow, they all ski the same. They don't ski reverse, none of them. I was watching we had here the other day the professional ski championships, the world championships. And here they all come, every one. You could hardly tell them apart. Molterer, who was winning, he made perhaps the most beautiful run I have ever seen. And where was he? Out, over the skis, with the skis. Rotation; not back here. Hinterseer, who wins the Olympic slalom, he never skis in reverse. He told me himself, 'I cannot do that. How do they do that?'

"And in that deep snow up there on Bell, what do you do when you get in that deep stuff? I see you. You ski rotation. You do not ski reverse. You were rotating. It is the same thing they all do when they get in that cruddy snow, or in that slush, where they need that power.

"Look, you can see all this in my book *The New Invitation to Skiing* [Simon and Schuster]. Have you read it? There I tell you how 'Toni Sailer, Anderl Molterer, Josl Rieder, Roger Staub

. . . were observed closely, not only training for races and in actual slalom and downhill racing, but skiing among themselves on Aspen Mountain for fun. While skiing among themselves, reverse shoulder action was virtually unseen. These men ski with great grace, elasticity, and power — and in every turn and motion it was always the "outside hand" that led the maneuver. Even the highest-speed short swings revealed a hint of rotation — and how else could it be? How can a skier have the forward aspect of the body and the intensely rapid action of the poles in *wedeln* with reverse shoulder action? The bumpier the terrain, the steeper the slopes, the rougher the conditions and the closer to the fall line the skiers went, the more apparent this became.

" 'Although each has his individual stylistic differences from the others, they were identical in the fact that they skied extremely lightly, with great elasticity and with "normal" technique as we have been expounding — that is, limited rotation is still visible in high-speed turns, and the skier's body is above and with the skis.

" '[With the reverse] the turn is initiated very hard, with a lot of skidding of the heels of the skis, and reverse shoulder action is employed to compensate for the overskidding. Put more simply and directly: if it were not for overskidding, the reverse shoulder action would constitute overcompensating.'

"That is what I say in my book. But I tell you, I like the reverse. People ask me and I say it is fine. I welcome it. Why? Competition, that is why. This fellow has his technique, and this one has his, and we have ours. And each one is always experimenting, working to beat the other one. And that is interesting. Besides, it makes good business for me. Because people go and they learn that reverse. Annie Taylor, that was in your magazine when you did those first articles with Willy Schaeffler. She was a good skier until she was ruined with that reverse. People learn that and pretty soon they are ruined, destroyed, and they come to me to save them. Sometimes maybe they would get down on their knees and beg with me, 'Please, please save me.' And I would say, 'No, go back. Not yet. Go back. You are not destroyed enough yet for me.' And then, when they have got themselves completely destroyed with that reverse shoulder technique, maybe they come back and we will save them."

A WORD FROM THE GENIUS

"I started all this reverse shoulder skiing in America," says Stein Eriksen (above), ski school director at Aspen Highlands. And it is true that Stein was the first man in the U. S. to really ski the reverse. At least it was obvious, when he raced in Aspen in 1950 as a member of the Norwegian national team, that he certainly was not rotating. It was equally obvious, for the next four or five years, that he was the best skier in the world. But nobody thought he was using any particular technique; they thought it was the genius in him. However, like most geniuses, Stein got that way by shrewd analysis and hard work. He was indeed skiing the reverse, and making his turns by a strong thrust of the legs and heels. But unlike the Kruckenhauser crew, he did not reverse as a counterforce for heel thrust. As Stein says, "The hip is the strongest part of the body, and therefore we should use it most for our skiing." When making a turn, Stein begins by reversing his shoulders — and hips — so that, as he comes through the turn, the entire body will be behind the hip as it presses forward and down on the outside ski, "so my whole ski is carving the turn, and I control that turn with the strongest part of me." Does it work? Watch him sometime.

FORGET THE RACERS

"Most systems are based on the experience of last year's star, and a racer's own winning style. What I'm concerned with is teaching people how to ski quickly, thoroughly, and yet confidently free from accidents." These are the words of Frank Day, no racer, but highly successful as a teacher at Sugarbush, Vt. "I really believe that I know how the ski is turned by the human body and leg structure. The basic functions of how a ski turns are based upon the fundamentals of how we turn a corner while we are walking. Teaching it becomes as simple as teaching walking. A turn may be broken down into five body-action parts. These five actions, the first being actually more of a static position, are: posture, facing, stepping, kneeling, and twisting. By learning these in sequence, at first separately, from a partially opened snowplow position [right], makes them easy to absorb. Then, by gradually bringing the skis closer together, and speeding up the motions, the five actions will blend, producing controlled, high-speed skiing. Throughout, the key to security is bending the knee forward and in."

REMEMBER THE RACERS

While some technique analysts, like Frank Day, say the worst thing to do is copy the racers, others say that all new and good things come from racing. This latter faction has a great many spokesmen, who became very noisy just after the 1960 Winter Olympics at Squaw Valley. At the Olympics, the Austrians did rather badly, and their defeat suggested that the Austrian method, *i.e.* the shortswing, was on the way out. What, then, was coming in? Some said the *schrittbogen,* or step-turn, in which the racer stepped onto the outside ski and swung through his turn carrying all but the tip of the inside ski in the air (left). However, this particular gambit turned out to be no technique but a racer's idiosyncrasy, and it suffered a swift demise at the hands of the weekenders and non-racing instructors who tried it.

PROJECTION CIRCULAIRE

Another answer to the Austrian recession was the renaissance of the French team. Skiers like Guy Périllat, Adrien Duvillard (right), Charles Bozon, and Jean Vuarnet (below) had begun the previous winter to creep up on the Austrians. At Squaw, they broke through and began winning medals, and they won with very little reverse shoulder. What did they use? In part they used a turn they called *Christiana Léger,* which really is a gentle form of rotation. Starting off in a square-shoulder, modern-Arlberg type of traverse, the skier comes up and forward from the knees, at the same time getting some extra lift with a forward swing of the outside arm. The shoulders do not move, but stay squared. The forward arm lift is called *projection circulaire,* which has become the rallying cry of a rejuvenated and renovated *Méthode Francaise* now being taught at a few American resorts.

ET LE PROFIL D'UN OEUF

The main French instrument of victory at Squaw Valley, however, was not a new turn but a faster way of going straight. The year before the Olympics, a tough little army man named Honoré Bonnet took over the French team, and charmed, bullied and trained it into a first-class competitive unit. Along the way he learned, largely from Vuarnet, the most intelligent ski technician on the team, that a skier in a streamlined crouch can go faster than a skier standing straight up. Vuarnet's crouch, shown left at the instant he crossed the finish line for his Olympic Downhill victory, made the skier's body look something like an egg. And that is the name the French gave their new position. Useless on a tight slalom course, and even more useless to a slow-moving recreational skier, the egg position has nevertheless become standard among all nations for downhill racing.

70

THE MOST HAPPY FELLA

The closing words of this seminar on ski technique will be delivered by the eminent Mr. Richard Durrance, America's first, oldest, and most delightful ski champion: "All this stuff about technique is bunk. I've got movies of the pro race — the world ski championships — and every damn one of them skis alike. Look, the whole idea is to have fun. Relax. Do what feels natural. Getting down the mountain, learning, learning to be safe — that's all fundamental. The variations are for afterwards." Thus endeth the entire lesson, except to say that Durrance's own way of getting down a mountain (below) is all variation. He bounces, he stems, he steps, he jumps, he snowplows, he sideslips, he whoops, he hollers, he rotates, and he reverses. The only constants are his joy in skiing and his scorn for technique nuts: "It's not supposed to be work; it's fun, for gosh sake."

PART II

CALL OF THE HIGH COUNTRY

There is almost nothing an American skier will not do to get a good run. In the East, he will pile into his car on Friday night and drive six to eight hours to sample the new powder on the Fall Line trail at Mad River Glen. In Jackson, Wyoming, he will get up on a morning when the temperature is a frightening 48 below zero to be at the foot of Snow King Mountain when the lift opens at 9:30. The four adventurers shown on the opposite page hired a helicopter and flew up to Utah's Mt. Timpanogos to try a slope that no one had ever skied before. And the platoon of diehards on page 75, crawling like so many ants to the rim of Tuckerman's Ravine, lugged their skis 2.3 miles up from the nearest road to take one last plunge before calling it a season. Wherever they go, and however they get there, U.S. skiers find some of the world's most beautiful terrain on which to practice their sport. On the following pages is a photographic sampling of this terrain, as well as the stories of the people who went to these—and other—mountains to create a complex of more than 300 resorts for the 2,000,000 Americans who can never seem to get enough skiing.

Photograph by Fred Lindholm for "Ski Magazine"

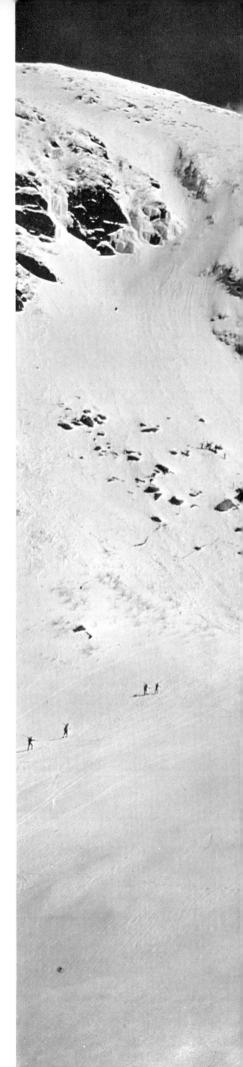

Jerry Cooke's camera records the quiet beauty of a winter morning at Mont Tremblant (above), while Ralph Crane captures the dramatic sweep of the massive headwall of Tuckerman's Ravine.

Swooping down toward a bank of clouds that half hides the distant surface

of Lake Tahoe, two skiers descend from Squaw Peak through new powder.

Photographs by Joern Gerdts

After a day of heavy traffic, Sun Valley's Exhibition Run turns into a sea of moguls. Even an expert must fight for balance as he bounces up over a crest and then down into a shaded gully.

In spring, the face of Mt. Hood becomes a vast highway where a skier can run for six miles, turning where he chooses, stopping only to rest or to admire the bold beauty of the high country around him.

CHAPTER 6

THE FAR CORNER

ITEM: It is 7:30 of a January morning on Mercer Island, Wash. A young housewife is holding a double boiler full of oatmeal in one hand, while with the other she gives a tug that frees the snagged zipper on her 9-year-old son's ski pants. The boy sits down to his breakfast, and the mother glances at the kitchen window where speckles of rain are beginning to blur the view across Lake Washington. She groans and walks, stiff-legged in her stretch pants and stocking feet, across the slippery linoleum floor to the phone. She dials a number and a wildly cheerful voice on the other end says, "Howdy, skiers; the daily weather report from the state highway department. Temperature thirty-three degrees. Snow mixed with rain. Compact snow and ice on the roads. Chains are required. Good skiing."

Is she downhearted? Does she peel off her stretch pants and go back to bed? Does she ship the boy off to the Saturday all-day movie? No. She leads him to the car and they plunge through the ghastly weather to the Cascade Mountains, where a moist and barely enduring ski instructor (left) takes over the boy while the mother climbs onto the chair lift for a glorious day of skiing.

ITEM: The evening of July 1. A girl has just taken her brother, who is visiting from the East, for a gentle, late-afternoon sail on the barely ruffled surface of the lake. They have a whiskey sour on the terrace, and the girl says, "Want to go skiing tomorrow?" "Sure," says the brother, and figures somebody must be kidding. But the next morning, at 3:45, it is woefully clear that no one was kidding. Out of the sack, into the car, four hours of driving — and there is the brother, rucksack full of lunch strapped to his back, climbing behind the girl through a cloud bank toward the invisible summit of the Mt. Baker massif. Later they ski off the edge of an abyss known as Table Mountain, and down the steep walls of Austin Pass, rattling over summer snow corrugated by rivulets of meltwater. At the bottom, the girl turns to wait for her sweating, staggering brother,

who finally pulls up, surprised and rather proud that he is still alive. The girl gives him a frosty sidelong stare. "Brother," she says, with true feeling, "I'm *very* disappointed in you." And she skis off; later she has to take the wheel herself and drive the exhausted man back to Seattle.

Cruel? Unusual? No, it is simply western Washington. And yes, it is simply western Washington. For this is a ski region like no other. It skis in the sun and in the rain. It skis in the winter and summer. It skis down cliffs, and it skis on level ground. And sometimes, as the pictures on pages 98–101 show, it skis on water, without benefit of tow boat.

Fifteen years ago, it barely skied at all. At that time, there weren't a half-dozen rope tows within 150 miles of Seattle. Today, there are 64 rope tows, a dozen chair lifts, two T-bars and six Poma lifts spread over eight major resorts and a hatful of lesser areas. They cater to something like 100,000 Seattle skiers and another 60,000 around the state of Washington. These figures do not include everyone with a dusty old pair of Northlands in the attic. They represent people who ski all winter, every winter: the housewives, who never miss the free Thursday ski school at Snoqualmie Summit; the doctors, lawyers, and dentists who beat the week-end mobs with a regular midweek visit to White Pass; the apple growers and other farmers from around Wenatchee who ski Stevens Pass while the earth is too frozen to work; the little kids who beg and cajole and practice until their mothers let them join Jack Nagel's racing classes (page 94); the college boys from Washington University who ski in snow-soaked levis, and the coeds who go for months without lunch so they can use the money to buy Bogner stretch pants and Meggi sweaters. It is a ski crowd like no other in the world, with a growth rate like no other — 10 to 15 per cent a year since 1946. And as the pictures and conversations on the next four pages will show, its history is as lively and improbable as the present.

83

With bold stride and bared shoulders, Walter Best of Seattle led the first ski ascent of Mt. Rainier in April, 1928.

"The Rangers Pulled a Raid"

Photographs courtesy Otto Giese

"We've had jumping and races out here since 1915," said Seattle ski veteran Otis Lamson, who shared some of the moments shown on these pages with his old racing and touring ally, Otto Giese. "But in those days nobody knew how to turn."

"They lined us up at the start like calisthenics," said Giese. "The Norwegians came out with jumping skis without poles, and I remember one guy had a football helmet and shoulder pads."

"There were no tows in those days," said Giese. "But there was a snow train on the Chicago, Milwaukee, and St. Paul Railroad that went through the Snoqualmie tunnel to a little town called Rockdale. Up above, at Beaver Lake, was a mountain climber's cabin put up in 1925 that we used for skiing in the winter. The trains left on Saturday night — we did the Big Apple all the way up — and they picked us up on Sunday. You had to burrow down through the snow to get to

continued

84

Ladies of the now defunct Summit Ski Club lined up at Cle Elum, Wash., in 1928, just before the club's 5th annual ski tournament. Six years later, the Seattle Junior Chamber of Commerce sent off 65 downhill racers all at once on Mt. Rainier. Fifth from right (below) in wild, "schmozzle" start is local ski historian Otto Giese, whose reminiscences, along with those of another early Northwest racer, begin at left.

Modern era in Northwest began in 1935 when National championships were held on Mt. Rainier. Eight thousand people watched Number 51, Hannes Schroll, laugh his way through both the slalom (above) which he won by 12.3 seconds, and the downhill (right), in which he finished 1.7 minutes ahead of his nearest rival, Dick Durrance of Dartmouth.

the cabins, and sometimes you'd find a bear in your snow tunnel. One night the forest rangers pulled a raid on us. Everyone was wrapped up in everyone else's sleeping bag. This was a shambles. Later we got an old boot and cut it up and awarded the ranger the Order of the Heel."

"Then," said Lamson, "in 1935 those Dartmouth guys and Hannes Schroll came out for the Nationals. That's when skiing really got started out here. The first rope tow went up two years later on Paradise Valley on Mt. Rainier in 1937. There was an old hotel up there. That's the only place in the U. S. that's gone backwards. The inn's fallen down—it's got squirrels and birds.

"There was a bus up to Stevens Pass then, too, though there weren't 100 skiers around. But it's sure different now. Heck, as late as 1952 I used to go up to Snoqualmie and see everybody I knew. Now, I look around and I realize there are thousands of people and I don't know any of them."

86

The Heroic Hills

In its growth, Seattle skiing has drawn its nourishment from two sources, both apparently inexhaustible: the people's enthusiasm for the sport, and the magnificent terrain close to the city. As an

Ray Atkeson

example of the latter, look at the picture above of Mt. Baker, a towering mass of volcanic rock buried under snow that is in places 70 feet deep. From its 10,750-foot summit, a network of glaciers tumbles down to seemingly endless snowfields and vast Alpine bowls. The season here starts about the first of November, ends officially with the Heather Cup slalom over the Fourth of

continued

July, and then wends its unofficial way to mid-September when the last diehard ski mountaineer comes huffing out of the deep ravine on the Southwest face of Table Mountain.

Nor is Mt. Baker the only place with magnificent terrain and a long, long season. At White Pass (left), the lifts open in November and keep going through May, when the skiers start touring the primitive area toward Hogback and the spectacular Goat Rocks region. The Olympic Peninsula, just across Puget Sound from Seattle, has at least four dozen peaks, as yet undeveloped, where the skiing need never really end; and back on the mainland, Mt. Rainier has almost limitless potential for spring skiers.

Why, then, doesn't everyone ski in western Washington? First, there are almost no overnight facilities. As a result, most of the ski business has always been local, daylight, week-end business: Snoqualmie closes down completely on Tuesday, and Stevens Pass closes on Monday, Tuesday, and most Fridays. As another result, there are no ski bums, and none of the sleek, *lamée* lizards who inhabit the inns of Aspen, Sun Valley, and Sugarbush, Vt. The young male skiers in the Seattle area are college boys out for the day, and the girls are more apple-pie pretty than slant-eyed and predatory — although, as the picture at right shows, there is nothing wrong with the local variety of apple pie.

The other thing that keeps the out-of-staters away is the rain that sweeps in from the Pacific and falls on everything west of the Cascade Divide. Each lift operator in the region claims his resort is in a rain shadow. The backers of the immense new ski area at Crystal Mountain proudly boast that they are in the rain shadow of Mt. Rainier, and therefore won't be half so wet as White Pass. While White Pass general manager Nelson Bennett boasted not long ago, "We're in the rain shadow of Mt. Rainier, and we don't get the stuff they'll get at Crystal Mountain."

Somewhere in the Cascades there may really be a rain shadow. Whoever finds it will need to hire a platoon of armed guards to fight off the eager mobs—and to take the money to the bank.

In early April, a trio of skiers swings down under the dark shoulder of Cathedral Rock, near White Pass; while, at right, a pretty climber hikes up the lower slopes of Mt. Baker for a run into Austin Bowl.

...And the No Less Heroic Skiers

Foremost heroes of Seattle ski campaigns are collegians who camp in snow, bus riders (below), and instructors like Snoqualmie's Marie Durant (right), whose ingenuity is limitless in dealing with weather.

But a little thing like a downpour, or no bed, never stopped a native Seattle skier. Some of the local college boys drive up on Friday and spend the night in sleeping bags laid out in gullies in the snow. Most of the skiers, however, sleep at home and go up to the mountains early in the morning. The number-one resort in terms of customers is Snoqualmie Summit, which each week end faces the onslaught of some 12,000 skiers. Sunday is the biggest day for adults, but it is Saturday that gives Snoqualmie its special flavor. That is the day when ninety-four buses disgorge the shattering total of 3200 skiing children. The PTA, the CYO, the Bellevue Ski School, the Mercer Island Ski School, the Ski Marina — everything but the Seattle Communist underground brings a busload of kids to Snoqualmie on Saturday morning for a daylong lesson. Mrs. George N. Prince, a Mercer Island mother who has seen it all, says, "You just can't *believe* Snoqualmie when those buses arrive. White Pass is farther away and it is not so crowded; but the thing at White Pass is getting hit. I've had my skis run over, and my boots cut, and I've been hit so hard it almost knocked me out."

White Pass, however, is not the only place where casualties are heavy. Each Monday, the Seattle *Times* publishes a week-end report that reads a little like the old communiqués from the Argonne. Here is the excerpted report of Jan. 29, 1962. "Spring skiing in January greeted thousands . . . over the week end. A warm sun shone much of the time. Ski Acres attracted 4,000 . . . the injured were Ellinor Patersen, 15, ankle; Diana Jones, 14, ankle . . . at Stevens Pass Warner Root, 16, suffered a hip dislocation. Hyak attracted 3,200 . . . the injured were Lee Strohm, 10, back injury." It got so bad at Stevens Pass one Sunday in 1961 that a pleading voice said, over the area's loud-speaker, "Please be extra careful for the rest of the afternoon. The first-aid infirmary is full, so we can't handle any more accidents today. Thank you."

Washington State News Bureau by Ted Bronstein

Nagel phones in countdown at start of girls' downhill.

A Skier's Gift to the Sport

Just after the 1960 Winter Olympics ended at Squaw Valley, there was a delightful little echo of the Games at Stevens Pass. It came in the form of a kids' Olympics, organized by a gas station operator named Jack Nagel, who is now director of the ski school at Crystal Mountain. Nagel was a member of the 1952 U. S. Olympic team, and for 10 years it has been his purpose "to give the sport a champion; I want to do something for skiing, because the sport has done so much for me." Part of this doing was the little Olympics at Stevens Pass, shown on these pages. But the major part of his repayment to the sport is his continuing program of training for children.

Three years ago Nagel looked around and discovered that the Seattle area was crawling with talented and highly competitive little skiers who participated in a scattering of junior events, but who had no regular coach and no single,

continued

Nagel's peewee Olympics had massive finish flags and all other trimmings of grown-up Winter Games. Youngest racers barely had chest area to display numbers. Though small, competitors never let up, either on race course (left) or at refreshment stand (below).

*Number of trophies far outstripped number of win-
ners. Above, youngest racer receives new ski parka.*

*Top finisher in junior girls' race flashes winning smile
as she stands next to Olympic flame, cradling trophy.*

*Parking lot attendant Steve Madison, known as the
"Mayor of Stevens Pass," tosses coins to youngsters.*

steady program of supervised races. So, in 1959,
he pulled the kids together into a gang he named
the Yellow Jackets, and he set up a yearly program of 20 days of training, with 10 scheduled
races. His original idea was to hold the Yellow
Jackets to a maximum of 60 racers, but already
he has nearly 100 future champions on his hands,
with dozens of others clamoring to get in. He
also has achieved his aim of giving the sport a
champion; and as the picture at far right shows,
he has done it in a most satisfying fashion.

96

A PERFECT GIFT

First lady of Jack's juniors, and finest gift a
father could give to a sport — or get from it —
is 15-year-old Cathy Nagel. In winter of 1962
she took leave of the racing classes, went
to Whitefish, Mont., as youngest entry in
National Junior championships, and won
ladies' downhill. In 1963, she won again.

Wild Finale for a Wonderful Season

When the Heather Cup race brings the season on Mt. Baker to its official end, a heavy crowd turns out — but not for the Heather Cup. They come to watch, and to enter, the kookiest skiing event in the United States, a completely spontaneous mixture of snow, sun, glacier water, and frozen blue bodies called the Slush Cup. At the bottom of Austin Bowl there is a tiny puddle of water called Terminal Lake. By the Fourth of July the sun has melted the icecap over the lake, and a deep, round, green puddle of 33-degree water bubbles up. The game is to climb the side of the bowl and then *schuss* down onto the lake, hoping you have enough speed to make a dry, stand-up run to the other side. Nobody ever wins the game. The few who actually make it across are rewarded by loud boos. Equipment is optional. Most contestants use regular skis, but some have tried air mattresses, rubber boats, shortie skis, water skis, ski-runner bicycles, and even canoes. They come down singly, in pairs, in trebles, with

continued

Photographs by Marshall Lockman

other skiers riding piggyback, and with screaming girls in their arms. Their costumes range from bathing suits to pajamas, shorts, *lederhosen,* cut-off jeans, tee shirts, cotton sweat shirts, floppy straw hats, long johns, and rubber wet suits. The greatest variety of all, however, is in the positions of the Slush Cuppers as, one after another, they gallantly fail to escape their icy dip.

CHAPTER 7

MT. HOOD MIRACLE

Six thousand feet up on the side of Mt. Hood near Portland, Ore., there is a ski resort called Timberline where, as the pictures on these pages show, it snows from time to time. This is not too unusual for the Pacific Northwest, a region which has never felt a lack of weather. There are, however, two things about Timberline that make it unique: (1) it has the only real ski hotel in the Northwest; and (2) for a time, a fair portion of Timberline's generous ration of snow was not out on the mountain where it could do no more harm than bury the chair lift, but was inside the resort's buildings, where it buried things like chairs, tables, beds, and the hopes of a good many Portland skiers.

In January, 1955, *Sports Illustrated* ran the following announcement in its weekly ski reports: "Mt. Hood, Ore., skiing excellent. U. S. Forest Service has canceled operating permit for Timberline Lodge, Inc., charging mismanagement,
continued

and a new operator is sought." The day after this announcement appeared in the magazine, the phone rang in the office of the ski editor and a voice belonging to Timberline's old manager said, "Your magazine ran a story that the Forest Service has closed Timberline. We're not closed at all. Now, you'll have to retract that statement, or we'll bring suit."

He was working with a fine point of law. For about a year, he had set some sort of world's record for mismanagement of a ski hotel, and the U. S. Forest Service, which controls the land around Timberline, had announced it was going to give him the old heave-ho. But the heave-ho did not become effective until several days after the announcement; and this was the fine point to which the manager was clinging. Obviously, a fat settlement from the magazine would soften the impact of his fall from the side of Mt. Hood. However, when he did hit the pavement at the expiration of a few days, there was no settlement to soften his landing, nor were any tears shed among the skiers of Portland at his demise.

He had started out selling popcorn from vending machines. With the popcorn profits, he picked up a small chain of movie theaters. He also picked up a number of civil suits, tax liens, and attachments. Although on several occasions fire damaged or destroyed his theaters — one of them three times — none of these little setbacks seemed to dismay the resilient manager, who sailed serenely along, paying small heed to the storms in his wake, and keeping a sharp lookout ahead for new places where he could exercise his unique talents.

He finally found a place, at Timberline, late in 1953. And what a place it was. The lodge itself was a mammoth affair, 360 feet long and four stories high, built by the WPA and the CCC during the Depression. It had rock walls as thick as a fortress. The 40-foot ceiling in the main lobby was held up by timbers 3½ feet in diameter. The furniture had been made by hand, and so had the railings on the staircase leading to the upper lobby, where hung a collection of paintings by the late, now-famed Depression artist, C. S. Price. There were dormitories and private rooms for 250 people, and in each room, the curtains and the upholstery for beds and chairs were hand-woven. The place was worth at least $5,000,000, not counting the mountain on which it stood, that being an 11,245-foot peak with year-round snow,

a chair lift called the Magic Mile, a rope tow, and an annual clientele of some 90,000 skiers from Portland only 47 miles away.

The former manager got the whole package for almost nothing. The previous lessees had poured money into the place a little faster than their potential profits justified, and were delighted to give both their stock — and their $80,000 in debts — to the manager when he offered to take them. As for the Forest Service, it was glad to have a hustling new man on the premises. "He was quite pleasant," said a Forest Service employee, "and he assured us he was going to build up Timberline."

As the months passed, however, it was a bit hard to see just what he was building. Nothing went up except the debt. The lease payments were met each quarter, but that was about the only money with which the manager seemed willing to part. No visible improvements were made (for a while the employees were being paid with

Leaning from window of Sno-Cat he uses to carry customers to top of Mt. Hood, Kohnstamm takes a satisfied look at the ski area which he changed from a filthy mess to a first-class resort.

for its wounded white elephant. For two months there was no keeper, and then, one day in March, a young man named Richard L. Kohnstamm volunteered to put the elephant back on his feet.

Kohnstamm had no previous experience in this kind of undertaking, but he had tons of money from the family chemical business. He also had a good heart (as certified by his degree in social work from Columbia University), and he liked skiing. Armed with these assets, and backed by a regiment of newly acquired help, Kohnstamm moved in on Mt. Hood.

"We knew things were bad up there," he told a *Sports Illustrated* writer later, "but we weren't prepared for what we found at the lodge. It's a work of art, you know, and it's hard to understand how anyone could treat it that way. There must have been a thousand fire violations. And the filth was almost indescribable. The grease was inches thick in the kitchen. We hired professionals — industrial cleaners — to clean the place from top to bottom, and even some of the professionals got sick, physically sick, at what they found in the rooms.

"And the destruction! Handwoven draperies had been used for rags and shoved into windows to keep the snow out because the panes were broken. The skiers' hut at the top of the chair lift — the Silcox Hut — was filled with snow, and some of the furniture there had been used for firewood."

Over the summer, Kohnstamm got the furniture back out of the fireplace, cleaned up the rooms, got the Magic Mile chair lift working again, and installed a $100,000 chair lift to serve the gentle slopes below the lodge. By winter the place was ready; so were the skiers, who came back in droves, once they realized the lodge was habitable. In the half dozen years since, Kohnstamm has established all sorts of Timberline precedents — like paying his bills, and spending money that he really had for sensible improvements. He has put in a $70,000 heated outdoor pool, and bought Sno-Cats to carry people to the upper slopes where, in late spring, they can start an 8-mile descent down to the bottom of the mountain. He has hired a couple of Austrian ex-

the money that came in to guarantee room reservations), and the service both inside the lodge and outside on the ski slopes deteriorated. Said one of the area's former directors, "People were coming to me and saying they would never go to Timberline again, the way they were treated and the way things were up there."

By the opening of the 1954-55 season, the place was in even worse shape. The lodge itself was a filthy mess. The chair lift wasn't working, and the local post office was holding a bunch of returned room keys on which the manager had refused to pay the 2¢ postage. Then, one cold January day, the electric company took a last weary look at Timberline's unpaid bills and pulled the switch that shut off the power.

As the lights went out in the lodge, the Forest Service finally woke up and invited the manager to scram. He did — a move which gratified everyone, but left the Forest Service with no keeper

continued

perts to teach in the ski school, and has pushed a late-season promotion called Austrian Week, during which there is much folk dancing, yodeling, beer drinking, skiing, and picnicking on the slopes. Total cost of the improvements to date is about $500,000, not counting a quarter of a million that Kohnstamm somehow mesmerized a local county organization into producing for a brand-new chair lift to replace the weather-beaten old Magic Mile.

Furthermore, while pouring in money, he has also poured in his own time and energy. "I've done just about everything around the lodge," he said not long ago. "Driven Sno-Cats farther than some of the Antarctic explorers — 43,000 miles. One evening I found out that our baker had quit, so I baked thirty-two pies so that we could have pie over the week end. Also the usual lift operating, desk clerking and houseman's jobs that most any innkeeper finds himself doing from time to time. I've done an awful lot of our own promotion work, including taking some pictures and writing copy for our brochures and ads as well as doing some of the work on a bunch of ski movies we've done here."

In sum, Kohnstamm feels, "I've gotten people to respect Timberline again." And indeed he

After blizzards, Timberline customers may have to dig for their cars, but Kohnstamm manages to keep them fairly happy with such extras as heated pool.

When the weather is right, Timberline is perhaps the most beautiful of all U. S. resorts. Best season is spring, when the upper mountain is open for touring.

has. However, he still faces a couple of problems. One is the absence of a regular profit, which even the scion of a chemical family would be glad to show. The other is the weather, which is no better at Timberline than it is at most other places in the Northwest. On warmish days, it rains on the lower slopes. On coldish days, it is likely to blow a gale across the upper mountain. On any day it is likely to snow, and keep on snowing until practically everything but the 750-pound bronze weather vane on the top of the lodge disappears from sight. But with Kohnstamm's prosperous hand on the helm, at least the weather is kept outside where it belongs, and whatever warmth there may be inside Timberline Lodge comes from the hearts of the satisfied customers rather than from the burning of hand-wrought WPA furniture.

CHAPTER 8
THE RECENT DAWN OF

108

HISTORY

Though skiing in Washington and Oregon has always been a thing apart, the history of recreational skiing elsewhere in the U. S. hangs together in a definite pattern. It began in Franconia, N. H., in December of 1929, with the opening of the first ski school in America (left). The rambling white building in the background is Peckett's, the first inn to attract a regular, out-of-state skiing clientele. And the man in the center, both at left and below, is Sig Buchmayr, the first man brought from Europe to teach skiing to Americans.

Buchmayr was dug out of the deep powder snow of the Austrian Alps in the winter of 1928 by a pair of American tourists, Mr. and Mrs. Grinnell Wylie, who invited him to visit them in New York. He did, and in the fall of 1929, he met Katherine Peckett, whose father owned an inn that needed some winter business. Sig moved to Franconia, set up a ski school, and brought in the business. "They ran that first year already one car of a snow train," said Sig, "that came all the way from New York."

In those days, there was no tow; the skiers just staggered up and down Sugar Hill, the slope in front of the inn; and there were no real mountain

continued

Sig Buchmayr (above) began by giving $1 ski lessons, now owns four sports shops with gross of $500,000.

First American ski tourists flounder through beginners' exercises on Sugar Hill in Franconia, N. H.

109

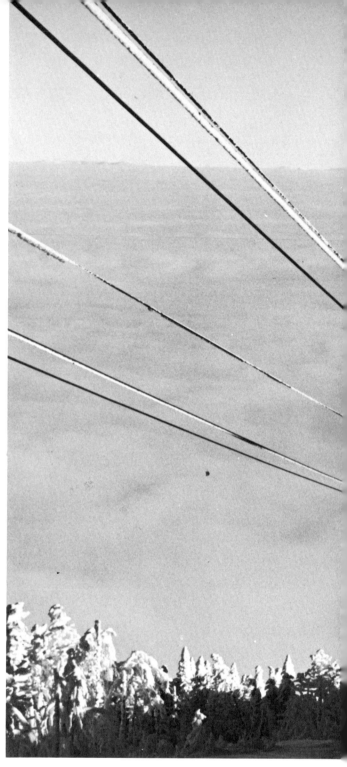

Alexander Bright (above) suggested first aerial tram in U. S. Later, operation of cable cars was directed by Roland Peabody (below), a local ski enthusiast.

trails to ski on. But that quickly changed. In 1932 the CCC cut the Taft Trail down the side of Cannon Mountain a few miles outside of town. This was a tough, sophisticated run, and it brought the skillful skiers of the Dartmouth College Outing Club to Franconia. On Dec. 22, 1935, a garage mechanic named Walt Poucher opened the first rope tow in town, and the tourists multiplied. Then, in September, 1937, thanks largely to the persuasions of a ski-minded Boston indus-

Rising above clouds in Franconia Notch, car carrying 27 passengers climbs 2022 feet in 5½ minutes to windy summit of 4017-foot Cannon Mountain.

trialist named Alexander Bright, the American Steel and Wire Co. started construction of an aerial tram, the first in America, to the top of Cannon Mountain. The winter the tram opened, 1938–39, it carried 36,589 riders; the next winter, 55,189. Over the next 13 years, 4 T-bars and 1 double chair were put up, and 17 miles of trails and open slopes cut on Cannon and adjacent Mittersill. In 1962 these facilities hauled 100,000 people uphill. And in the season of 1963, with the addition of 1 more chair, another T-bar, and an additional 40 more acres of open slopes, the town of Franconia, which was the first to cater seriously to ski tourists, had as many modern facilities, and perhaps as many customers during the winter season as any other area in the U. S.

111

Vanguard
of an Army

Despite the goings-on in Franconia, prior to the winter of 1932 most adults in the U. S. thought of snow as something to be either avoided or shoveled. Then at 10 A.M. on Feb. 4 at Lake Placid, N. Y., the Adams Empire State Band struck up "The Star-Spangled Banner," and a parade of winter sports athletes from 17 nations, among them the American team (right), swung past in review. As the last team went by, Governor Franklin D. Roosevelt stood up and said, "I proclaim open the Third Olympic Winter Games." From that moment on, winter sports became something that Americans cared about. Eighty thousand people – including Admiral Byrd, who was scouting for potential Arctic explorers – sloshed around in the rain and melting snow during the ten days of the Games, and howled with joy as the U. S. swept the speed skating and bobsledding to win 6 of the 14 events. Millions of others saw the Games in newsreels, or heard them described on the radio.

Along with the drama of the Olympics, there was an aura of commerce, of politics, of confusion, and of plain bad luck that has never deserted the Winter Games. Lake Placid had decided to bid for the Games to give the place a boost in winter tourism. Then, before it could build facilities, Placid had to grope its way through a forest of lawsuits and legislative hocus-pocus, not the least of which was the extraction of $500,000 from the New York legislature for expenses. Once the money was in hand, there was a panic about getting the ice arena finished in time (they made it by exactly 10 days). And of course the weather was awful. The winter of 1932 was the warmest in the history of the New York weather bureau; the entire bobsled run washed out twice.

But somehow, as it always has, the Winter Olympics opened on time. Mrs. Roosevelt showed her confidence in the bob run by taking a ride on opening day. And despite sun, rain, politics, and commerce, the 1932 Olympics were a success, not only in the competitive events, but as a means of getting America interested in winter sports.

Onward & Upward

Once people got interested in skiing, they began to look around for some way, other than walking, of getting uphill. In the winter of 1934, they finally got it. Their benefactor was Bunny Bertram, ex-captain of the Dartmouth ski team, who picked up the idea of a continuous rope lift from fellow skier Douglas Burden, and passed it on to Robert Royce, an innkeeper in Woodstock, Vt. Royce, no dope, hustled out and rented the handiest slope, Gilbert's Hill, for $10 for the entire season. "Then," says Bertram, "before I knew it he had David Dodd, the sawmill mechanic, out there working." When Dodd finished, he had built the first permanent ski lift (above) in the U. S., a 1000-foot rope run off the wheel of a jacked-up Model T — rather, off five jacked-up Model T's, since that was the number of transmissions Dodd's contraption burned out the first season.

The Happy, Horrible Rattlers

Although at least one railroad still runs a shiny, diesel-powered special it calls a snow train, the true snow train (below) flourished in the Thirties and died in the early Fifties. Historically, a snow train was a ghastly old rattler pulled by a steam locomotive along an almost abandoned section of track. The most famous of the early Eastern trains was one that the Boston and Maine ran to New Hampshire in the winter of 1931–32. It left Boston each Friday with about 200 happy, hard-drinking regulars, and uncoupled a car or two for the week end at places like Intervale, Warner, and Plymouth. The passengers were so happy and so regular that some of the other railroads, notably the New York Central, hastened to cut in on the action. In attendance on a typical Central train was a sporting goods clerk named Ernie Blake (see page 210). "Another boy and I used to run that train for Saks Fifth Avenue," said Blake recently. "The New York Central had a useless spur, and I guess they wanted to promote business. We went to North Creek, in the Adirondacks. This was a fabulous resort — one rope tow, and then we went to the top of the mountain in an old Ford. We stayed at farmhouses. The train had a bunch of old-fashioned sleepers, a bar car, and a car where we sold wax and goggles, and rented horrible equipment. Skiing was not so sophisticated then." But it is now, and people go up in their automobiles.

CHAPTER 9

THE SECOND COMING

During the middle Thirties, there was only one name in skiing, and it belonged to Hannes Schneider, the hawk-faced Tyrolean who had founded the Arlberg ski school. In Austria, in fact all through the Alpine countries, Schneider was every kind of hero. He had fought with the Austrian army in Russia and on the Italian front. After the war, he had won a hatful of skiing championships, including, in 1922, first prize in the German Winter Sport competitions. That same year he founded his ski school at the Hotel Post in St. Anton, and by 1925 the Post had become winter quarters for sports-minded royalty, deposed and otherwise, wandering the Continent. When Hannes roared, *"Kniee beugen!"* King Alfonso of Spain and King Albert of Belgium bent their knees. And when Prince von Starhemberg of Austria blundered into other pupils on the slope, Schneider advised them to "hit him on the head."

While thus impressing royalty, Hannes also wowed the peasantry by his performances in a series of ski films. He became a living god of winter; and when America discovered winter as something to be wondered at rather than avoided, the call went out for Hannes to come over and be worshiped.

The first coming of Hannes was to Boston in early December, 1936, to put on a ski exhibition during a winter sports show at the Boston Gar-
continued

Hannes got a hero's welcome in 1939 as he walked down the North Conway station platform with assistant Benno Rybizka. Since Schneider's death in 1955, the ski school has been run by his son Herbert.

117

den. There, Hannes slid up and down a wooden slide covered with shaved ice. Two weeks later, he went through the act again at Madison Square Garden, then left for Austria, firing this majestic salute in his wake: "American skiing still needs lots of organizing; the wave came so suddenly that nobody could take hold of it, but a few years from now it probably will look different when the public insists on good ski schools." This shot caught the Norwegian instructors established at Lake Placid just below the waterline, and they fired back: "There is nothing in the skiing technique of Schneider which is new to Norwegians. The skiers at home considered it a mark of cowardice to snowplow, and everyone can make

the turns on which Schneider puts so much importance."

If he managed to touch off the first ski technique war in America, it was nothing to the war he found when he got home. Hitler was on the move; within 18 months there was no more Austria and very nearly no more Hannes. Just after the *Anschluss,* Hannes was tossed in jail and deposed not only as head of his own Arlberg school, but also from his far more influential job as head of all Austrian ski certification. There was considerable wailing and gnashing of teeth among American skiers when Hannes was interned, and a few American skiers decided to do something about it. The most effective was Harvey Gibson, a native of North Conway, N. H., who had become president of the Manufacturer's Trust in New York.

In the winter of 1937–38, Mr. Gibson decided to make a major ski resort out of his old home town. There already was a branch of the Arlberg ski school in North Conway, owned by a ski pioneer named Carol Reed and run by one of Hannes' loyal instructors, Benno Rybizka. Gibson bought the school from Reed, bought and remodeled an old hotel, had a local lumberman cut trails and open slopes on Lookout Mountain (now Mt. Cranmore), and installed Reed as operator of a Saks Fifth Avenue ski shop. Then Gibson reached across the ocean into the German Ministry of Finance, and got its director, Hjalmar Schacht, to spring Hannes.

The great man arrived at the North Conway Railroad Station at 7:00 A.M., Feb. 12. By ten o'clock he was skiing, and by the following fall, he felt there was now hope for U. S. skiing: "In three years, American skiing should reach a standard comparable to that in Europe."

Cranmore Skimobile, opened in time for Hannes' arrival, was brainchild of Conway garage mechanic George Morten, and is still in operation today.

CHAPTER 10

A PLACE IN

THE SUN

Dashing Count Felix Schaffgotsch discovered location for Sun Valley in a sheep pasture in Idaho. Later he returned many times as a guest. Here he is shown with movie star Madeleine Carroll on his arm.

Once upon a time, in 1935 to be exact, there was a broad meadow in the mountains of central Idaho that was very empty. Boy, was it empty — empty even of the building shown in the photograph at left. Late each spring, a bunch of men would come out from Ketchum — not very many men because there were only 150 people in Ketchum — to round up the sheep that roamed the meadow, and ship the lambs down the least profitable rail spur in the entire Union Pacific empire to the town of Shoshone on the UP's main line. That was pretty much all that happened around this valley.

Then, one bitter February afternoon in 1936, an Austrian count, a suave character named Felix Schaffgotsch, came mushing up the road. Like the valley, the count had fallen on slow times. His family owned a fat slice of the high and beautiful Riesengebirge section of Austria. "But," said the count, sadly, "this land belongs to my uncle, who is head of the family." Thus the count, a sometime skier, was by no means of-

continued

fended when his old acquaintance, UP Board Chairman Averill Harriman, came to him with a proposition: Would the count survey all the vast territory serviced by the UP for a place to put "a ski center in the mountains here of the same character as in the Swiss and Austrian Alps?" He could take the whole winter if he wanted, and the railroad would cover all his expenses. Would the count consider this favor? Would he ever.

He arrived in New York on Dec. 2, 1935, and headed straight for the West. (Harriman had written, "I understand skiing in the East is not very good.") His first port of call was Paradise Valley (see pages 144–145) on the side of Mt. Rainier, where he stayed a week, skied, and basked under the solicitations of local ski dignitaries. He was so happy that he seemed about to give his blessing to Mt. Rainier as the site for the UP's winter playground. Had he done so there would have been rejoicing among his escort of railroad officials, several of whom were less than dazzled by the entire boondoggle. But, alas, Mt. Rainier was national forest land, and, said the count, with the true aristocrat's sense of popular responsibility, "You cannot take the mountain away from the people. I intend," he continued grandly, "to visit all the skiing grounds in the country before I leave."

The next skiing ground he surveyed was Mt. Hood, upon which torrents of rain were falling at the time. The count refused even to get out of

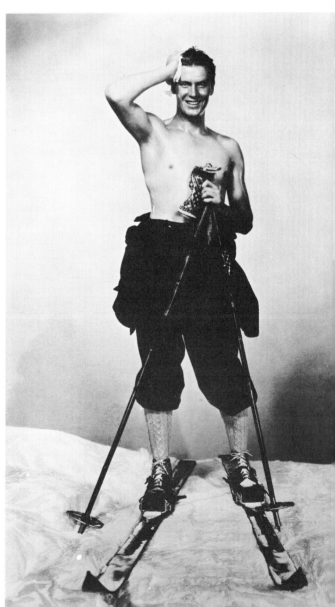

As part of promotion, Hannegan smeared boy model with Vaseline, posed him at New York studio on indoor snowscape of cotton and gauze, told newsmen the photo showed typical winter fun in Sun Valley.

In March, 1936, Steve Hannegan (above, right) told a handsome young Averill Harriman exactly what to build; within a month, construction was started on America's first major-league winter sports resort.

World's first chair lift, opened on Dollar Mountain in December, 1936, was designed by UP bridge engineer James Curran as adaptation of banana-boat loading tram. In its very first test, lift broke down.

the car. Thence to Yosemite, which was nice, but it, like Rainier, "belonged to the people." Next, to Colorado — "too windy and cold." Then Utah — "too dark." Then, by horsedrawn sleigh over Teton Pass to Jackson, Wyo., which the count pronounced perfect. In fact, Sun Valley would be there today, except that Jackson had no railroad and the Wyoming highway department wouldn't promise to keep the road plowed over the pass. Finally, on that bitter February day, with the wind moaning through the Sawtooth Range, piling drifts neck deep along the road, the count was hauled rather reluctantly to the end of the line on the Ketchum spur.

He took a quick look at the place and was swept with an almost overpowering urge to leave. Ketchum registered the same enthusiasm for Schaffgotsch. Told that an Austrian count was in town looking for a place to build a million-dollar hotel, Jack Lane, a local sheepman, glanced up from his lambing chores and said, "Don't cash any of his checks." The count, however, was not hurting for cash at this point, and he stayed a

while. After refreshing himself with a meal of bread, canned peaches, and coffee bought at Griffith Brothers, the only store in town, Count Schaffgotsch said: "These hills look pretty good. Get me someone who can ski." A teen-age boy stepped forward, equipped à la Snowshoe Thompson, with huge boards and one pole. With the boy as guide, Schaffgotsch set off, up the back side of one of the mountains and down into the broad meadow, which was part of the Brass Ranch.

He liked the meadow, and called for a deck chair. For the next few days, he did nothing but sit in the chair, moving it occasionally until he found the spot which the sun reached first in the morning and left last in the afternoon. When he found it, he wired Harriman: THIS IS THE PLACE. Dutifully, Harriman hitched up his private car, came to Ketchum, and instantly caught cold. He also caught the count's enthusiasm. After summoning Charlie Proctor, captain of the 1928–29 Dartmouth ski teams, to give the place a final O.K., Harriman gave the word to buy. This the UP did — 43,300 acres for little more than taxes.

With the location chosen and the land bought, Harriman still had a few little problems, like what was he going to do now, and who would

continued

Hans Hauser came to Sun Valley to teach skiing, learned a thing or two himself before return to Europe.

Claudette Colbert, on hand for opening, was one of Hollywood stars who began skiing at Sun Valley.

New Yorker Margaret Emerson found Sun Valley a good place to relax, an easy place to make friends.

possibly care once he did it? To answer these questions, he called in a publicity wizard named Steve Hannegan. Not long before, Hannegan had promoted a worthless stretch of sand dunes into a resort called Miami Beach. But even Hannegan's bold spirit momentarily failed when he first beheld the spot which Schaffgotsch had described as having "more delightful features than any place I have seen in the United States, Switzerland or Austria, for a winter sports resort."

"We went up the line in a covered handcar," said Hannegan later, "and looked around, and all I could see was a goddam field of snow. I thought they must be crazy. 'This is strictly ridiculous,' I said. But we walked around some more, with my shoes full of snow, and then the sun came out. It began to feel pretty good, so I opened my coat. Then I took it off. Pretty soon I opened my vest. Then I began to sweat. When you think of winter sports you usually think of cold, don't you? Well, I always believed in a good name. We had a lot of trouble that way with Miami Beach being so near Miami. I always said if I started a town there, I'd call it Sunshine, Florida." Whereupon he christened the UP's remote, snow-filled meadow "Sun Valley, Idaho." Then he sat down to tell Harriman, in a letter, what to build.

"It must be a complete unit of entertainment," he wrote, "with full facilities for winter sports enjoyment." Besides a first-class hotel, there "should be an ice rink, a glass-walled but open-ceilinged hot-water pool, a billiard parlor, a bowling alley, a motion picture show, a toboggan slide, a few dog teams. Mechanical devices must be installed which will take people to the top of the slides.

"Although the very nature of the community being established makes it selective, it will be necessary to further restrict clientele through careful perusal of reservation requests. We must be careful to get our style and our tempo from the very first.

"If it is not done on this scale, it should not be done at all."

Harriman decided to go the whole route, and, in April, ground was broken for the main lodge, with Hannegan's other enumerated creature comforts to follow. The lodge was finished in seven months, and it was finished in a style seen nowhere else on this earth. A massive thing made to accommodate 288 guests and 124 employees, its exterior walls were reinforced concrete dyed

Dick Durrance won first Harriman Cup, then won again two years later despite injured foot which he soothed on eve of race with external applications of warm water and internal treatments of cold beer.

with an ochre stain and poured into forms of rough-sawed bull pine so that the cement, as it hardened, picked up the grain of the wood. As for the pool, when the man who owned the hot springs from which the UP wanted to pipe in real mineral water for the pool held out for $150,000, the UP warmed up its own local well water into which it periodically tossed an ersatz brew of minerals. Harriman's own private cottage, not started until cold weather had set in, was built in 60 days inside a heated circus tent. This was nothing, however, to the pure genius that went into the ski lifts.

At this point in ski history, there were cable
continued

Shah of Iran peeled fruit during descent of Baldy.

Esther Williams tried kick turn on Dollar Mountain.

Ski school head Sigi Engl shows Burt Lancaster how.
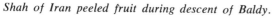

cars for big mountains and rope tows for small slopes. But nobody had yet invented a safe, fast, comfortable way to get lots of people up medium-sized mountains, such as surrounded Sun Valley. Well, said the UP's bridge engineer, James Curran, how about rigging up something like the endless cable he had once designed to unload bananas from fruit boats, and replacing the banana hooks with chairs? Most of the railroad brass thought that was the worst idea they had ever heard, but Board Chairman Harriman thought perhaps it wasn't. In the first test of the chair idea, a friend of Harriman's named John E. P. Morgan strapped on his skis and stood on a pile of straw while a chair slung from the side of a small truck approached from the rear for a pickup. This was not a success. Morgan got up, substituted roller skates for skis, and tried it again, on concrete. Fortunately, this time he made it. That was good enough for Curran, who charged out to Sun Valley to put one chair lift on
continued

June Allyson scolded skis as she tried snowplow.   *Leonard Bernstein struck sour note in first recital.*

Ski enthusiast Gary Cooper caught olive tossed by Sun Valley resident Ernest Hemingway, a good party man.

Dollar Mountain in front of the lodge, and another on Proctor Mountain behind it.

While the lifts were going up, the exuberant Curran broke his arm in an impromptu skating race on the just-completed ice rink, and thus missed riding on the chair the day the lift was turned on. It was just as well, for, in mid-test, a fuse blew, leaving a group of lady volunteers swinging dizzily from their chairs. By the time the last passenger had been brought down, the lift was working again, but none of the girls was about to get back on. None, that is, until the valley's new manager gave his secretary, Florence Law, a choice of two rides: up Dollar Mountain on the lift or out of town on the next train.

On December 21, 1936, Sun Valley opened. Everybody was there, Hannegan saw to that — Sam Goldwyn, Tommy Hitchcock, Robert Young, Claudette Colbert. Harriman was there, and Hannegan himself, and Hans Hauser, the big, good-looking Austrian ski champion who had been brought over with five cronies to run the Valley's ski school. Of course the place was full of reporters. In fact, Sun Valley was full of everything except snow. Thirty-six years of U. S. Government weather data to the contrary, there was not a flake in the valley. To those guests who had still not arrived, Harriman wired: "No snow here. If you are a good gambler, come on out and be our guest until it arrives." Hannegan, however, fell back on a higher power. On Christmas Eve, he took himself to mass and prayed. Later that night, as the publicity man sat morosely by his window, snow began to fall. Hans Hauser, ecstatic, ran into the whitening night and shouted, *"Schnee!"* Hannegan ran to the bar, acquired a bottle of champagne, and passed the night alone in his room, happily sipping as he watched the thick flakes drift into the valley.

It snowed for four days. Then, on New Year's Eve, Hannegan was blessed again. During a party, David O. Selznick popped investment banker Charles F. Glore in the eye. Hannegan spread the word all over the country. "Sun Valley Opens With a Bang" said the New York *Herald Tribune,* with pictures of the two celebrated combatants and their ladies.

From that wild and wonderful opening, Sun Valley went on to become everything that Harriman, Hannegan, or the growing number of American ski tourists could possibly want. The names from society, Hollywood, and big business kept pouring in: Gary Cooper, Robert Pabst,

Norma Shearer, Ernest Hemingway, William S. Paley, Lydia duPont, J. M. Studebaker, Julius Fleischmann, Clark Gable. Some came to ski, some to party, some to gamble, some to sit out Idaho's easy divorce requirements (six weeks' residence and $500 minimum legal fee). Some of the ladies declared open season on ski instructors, a species of North American big game which, like the pronghorn antelope, has grown and flourished despite increasing hunting pressure and appalling casualties. Among the first to fall was Friedl Pfeifer, to Hoyt Smith, a Salt Lake City heiress. Another was Marty Arrougé, who has stayed happily married these 20 years to Norma Shearer.

Perhaps the most fascinating trophy, thanks more to the hunter than to the hunted, was Hans Hauser, who now decorates the living room of a lady named Virginia Hill. Miss Hill, later to win renown through her disclosure to a senate committee of her friendship with the mob, swept into Sun Valley one day in the company of a girl friend and a maid. She threw endless parties, bought cartons of clothes, hired Hans Hauser by the week. Everything was paid for with hundred-dollar bills and keep the change. Each week a new supply of hundreds would arrive wrapped in a shoe box, presumably from the associates of her late boy friend Bugsy ("I always call him Benjamin") Siegel. Finally, to the immense relief of the UP, Miss Hill left for Aspen, but took Hans Hauser with her, still under hire. The happy couple surfaced once more when Miss Hill was called before the McClellan Rackets Committee, and then vanished to Switzerland where they now live in wedlock with their son.

Meanwhile, back at the old Brass Ranch, Steve Hannegan was finding more angles than Harriman had dreamed possible. He persuaded Paramount Pictures to use Sun Valley as a location for *She Met Him in Paris.* (Since then, two other complete movies and dozens of location shots have been made there.) He coined the term "snow tan," and to prove you could get one he

continued

Piles of skis and suitcases awaiting departure of Snowball Limited from Union Station in Los Angeles signified success of postwar change in Sun Valley promotional policy. Along with big names, Valley now welcomed big crowds of real skiers.

128

The high peaks of the beautiful and still wild Sawtooth Range form a backdrop for a skier starting
down Baldy. Sun Valley bulldozes and seeds its slopes
so the skiing stays good from December to April.

After a day of hard skiing on Baldy or Dollar Mountain, a clutch of happy guests relaxes in the glass-walled, heated pool where waiters bring cold martinis to the steaming swimmers. In mid-swim, the bravest of the bathers try a quick dip in the snow outside the glass walls to get blood moving again.

hired a New York photographic studio to fake an immensely successful picture of a young man supposedly having a warm, wonderful time skiing in Sun Valley. (Hannegan himself always had a horrible time in Sun Valley; he caught cold whenever he went near the place.) And he made it impossible for anyone but a slob to stay in Sun Valley without having a smiling photograph appear in the visitor's hometown paper. As for the real slobs, they were kept to a minimum by the reservations policy, and by a squad of four railroad detectives who drifted unobtrusively through the lodge.

As Hannegan pushed, the UP built: the Challenger Inn for 230 guests who might want Sun Valley for something less than lodge rates ($48 for a suite to infinity for the Harriman Cottage); a camera shop, drug store, beauty parlor, and movie house; a post office, the Ram Bar, the Aspen and Willow guest cottages, and a greenhouse to supply free flowers to guests; two multiunit skiers' chalets, another swimming pool, a big new chair lift on nearby Baldy Mountain, and shuttle bus service to and from the lifts; plus golf, tennis, riding, and trap and skeet shooting for summer visitors. It was a big, happy retreat where a guest needed nothing more than his room number as a credit card, and it cost the UP an

continued

annual deficit of an estimated $750,000 to keep it that way.

Then, in 1949, the UP got a new president named Arthur Stoddard (Harriman was long gone into politics) who sent out a stiff memorandum on the losses at Sun Valley. That was the end of the froufrou — and of lodge manager Pat Rogers, who resigned in despair when Stoddard decreed that the UP would no longer bestow extravagant favors on its skiing guests. Sun Valley now began to push things like the country's first

In best Steve Hannegan tradition, Sun Valley photographer Fred Lindholm scales tall evergreen, straps himself precariously to tree to get better shot.

Jazz trumpeter Louis "Satchmo" Armstrong leads downhill charge by elite skiers of professional racing circuit. Gagging it up with old Satch are, from left, Anderl Molterer, Christian Pravda, Pepi Gramshammer, Roger Staub, Stein Eriksen (note fur-topped boots), Les Streeter, and Ulaf Skaeringsson of Iceland.

Learn-to-Ski Weeks ($75 per week for room, board, lift, and lessons), $3 dormitory accommodations, and special snow trains from Los Angeles and Chicago. The Valley became less a place to see, and more a place to ski. The ski school itself, under the wise leadership of a bright little Swiss named Sigi Engl, found itself teaching 700 people out of a weekly visitor count of about 1000. The slopes of Dollar Mountain were graded and groomed till they became the world's best for beginners and intermediates. Skiing on Proctor Mountain became largely a memory, but the new runs on Baldy were enough to keep any expert happy.

Sun Valley now manages to break about even, which is what Stoddard wants. However, while soliciting the herd to help in its rise from the red, the Valley has by no means lost its class. The lodge is still about the most comfortable non-private pad in American skiing. Favored guests still get free flowers. Famous people still pop up with fair regularity: not long ago the Shah of Iran arrived with a bodyguard who carried a huge revolver; since the guard never left the Shah and also could not ski three feet without falling,

continued

Photographs by Fred Lindholm

Austrian instructor Conrad Staudinger comes up after a long dive through deep powder.

Sun Valley today is filled with pretty girls who ski better, look better than old-time movie stars. Above, Sydney Lindholm swings through a turn; while, below, Hildegard Flagg carves traverse on Baldy.

the Shah's instructors refused to permit His Majesty on the mountain until the guard's gun was emptied of bullets.

The lodge retains an atmosphere that is utterly unique in the otherwise rough-and-ready ski territory of the Northwest. There are bellhops who run out to park a visitor's car. There are ancient women playing cards in big, dark lounges. Less ancient women drift around in slim, tailored slacks and Pucci shirts. There's a strong smell of Arpège and martinis. There are rules about neckties. Austrian ski instructors are on hand with their sharp red faces, sharp black shoes, blue suits and very white shirts. Mink coats, high heels, a broad or two, and several broads *emeritus*. A band in the plush Duchin Room won't stop playing "Sun Valley Twist," the words of which seem to be "Sun Valley Twist," or, alternatively, "Let's all twist," or just "Twist," and of which Dorice Taylor, who inherited the Valley's publicity bureau from the late Steve Hannegan, says bravely, "We think this is the best twist of all."

Whirling down the back side of Baldy, three instructors take a wild ride on typical Sun Valley ski slope.

CHAPTER 11

A PLACE FOR PROS

In 1938 another Western ski area struggled into being — an area not far from Sun Valley but utterly unlike it. Its name was Alta, Utah, and it was no place for social skiers or tourists.

The Alta of 1938 was a canyon, hemmed in by wild, steep mountains. Upon these mountains fell at least 40 feet of snow a year, some of the lightest, fluffiest powder in the world. But once the snow fell, it had very little to cling to on the treeless upper slopes; after a particularly heavy storm, tons of it would go rumbling down in avalanches like the one shown below. For years there was no one to marvel at the snow or worry about the avalanches but a bunch of lead and silver miners, 60 of whom were killed in one hor-

rifying series of snowslides in 1874. By the '30's, the population of Alta was very low indeed. It consisted of one forest ranger, who kept his eye on that cold neck of the Wasatch National Forest, and a man named George H. Watson.

Mr. Watson had a cabin which in times of deep snow could be entered only through a kind of wooden chimney. There in his burrow he dreamed of restoring the silver-mining glories of the old days. To that end, he scraped up a patchwork of 1800 acres' worth of old mining claims, and struck a bargain with the Wasatch foresters. If the government would build a road for the ore trucks that Mr. Watson would be running, he would turn over the surface rights to his acres so

continued

Tons of Alta's famous powder snow crack loose and rumble across ski tracks on treeless upper slopes.

At apex of great horseshoe of hills that forms Alta's ski terrain, two instructors take off through deep snow.

Color photograph by John G. Zimmerman

In spring, after snow has stabilized, Joern Gerdts'
camera catches five skiers skittering down avalanche

gullies shown on preceding page. These gullies, called the "Chutes," are among steepest runs in U. S. No lift services them; anyone brave enough to try them must make long, tricky climb to the jumping-off place.

Photographs by Fred Lindholm

the Forest Service could develop the canyon for recreational use. No new miners ever came up the road, but a lot of other people did.

The first to come was a group of Salt Lake businessmen, who arrived in 1938 with the paraphernalia to convert an old mining tram into a skier's chair lift. Next came the Denver and Rio Grande Western Railroad with $25,000 to start building a lodge, hopefully a Sun Valley sort of lodge. Then came a Dartmouth racer named Dick Durrance, with an Eastern friend, James Laughlin, head of a small, adventurous publishing house since grown famous as New Directions. Together they finished building the lodge, which was never going to be anything like Sun Valley, and of which the Denver and Rio Grande swiftly despaired. Durrance ran the ski school, Laughlin, among other things, saw to the construction of another small lift above the chair, and between them they operated the lodge.

From the beginning, their customers were dead serious skiers who could handle themselves in deep powder, and relished a plunge down the Chutes (pages 140–41). They were also willing to limit their night life to a couple of beakers of old man Watson's special brew — hot bourbon flavored with spruce needles. Since then, the essence of Alta has changed very little. True, new lifts have gone up. Two other lodges, the Rustler and the Peruvian, have been built. The forest ranger is now a snow ranger, who studies avalanches and works major miracles in predicting or preventing the worst slides. Last summer, still another chair went up, which Laughlin claims "opens lots of rolling terrain for beginners." But despite these civilizing moves, the snow still falls 40 feet a year; the avalanches — despite constant surveillance and heroic control measures — still roar down, closing slopes and blocking the road up from Salt Lake; and the powder-loving experts hope the words of Alta's general manager *emeritus* Fred Speyer will always apply: "Look. To make money you got to have snow bunnies — beginners. How can I make money? All I got here is skiers."

Alta has made such gestures toward civilization as heated pool, new wings on Alta and Rustler Lodges, a new lift to service easier terrain. But basic appeal of rugged Utah resort is still its bottomless snow and hair-raising expert runs like High Rustler (right).

CHAPTER 12

FROM PARADISE TO THE PO

When World War II began, everyone who skied, or thought he could, headed for Fort Lewis outside Tacoma, Wash. There, the 87th Mountain Infantry Regiment had just been reactivated — at first only on paper — to form the nucleus of the first division of ski troops in the history of the U. S. Army.

The first recruit to arrive was, naturally, a Dartmouth skier named Charley McLane, who asked a sentry where the ski troops were. Baffled, the sentry checked with the brass and then returned to inform McLane thus: "Mister, you're the ski troops." When the regiment filled up, it moved in midwinter to Tatoosh and Paradise Lodges on Mt. Rainier for snow training. The officers tried hard to keep things military, but there was too much snow outside to hold formations and the lobby and corridors were too small to do it inside. So finally they just skipped formation, got up like civilians around 7:30, and spent most of the day skiing. Other skiers got the good word and hastened to join, but by the time they arrived the inns were full and the new recruits were stuck in a mule company down in Yakima.

The following fall, the growing division moved to new quarters at Camp Hale, Colo., where, as the 10th Mountain Div., it set a record for long-haul training without firing a gun in anger. During this period, it carried out the infamous Retreat from Red Mountain, wherein a detach-
continued

Happiest days for 10th Mountain were in winter of 1942, spent near Paradise Lodge on Mt. Rainier.

145

ment on maneuvers between Aspen, Colo., and Camp Hale became hopelessly lost on Red Mountain. The officer in charge gave up and spent the night snugly bedded down in Aspen's Hotel Jerome while his men, frostbitten and furious, stumbled back to town as best they could. Later, this same officer delighted his company by breaking his arm in a fall from a tree while showing how to clear a field of fire.

The *opéra bouffe* ended in January, 1945, when the 10th Division landed in Italy to take on some of the toughest elements of the *Wehrmacht* in the worst kind of mountain terrain. From the beginning, the green division fought with inspired gallantry, scaling seemingly impossible, ice-covered cliffs and working miracles of transport, to help drive the Germans up the spine of Italy and across the Po River to the foothills of the Alps. There, on May 2, the war in Italy came to a close, and the 10th put down its guns, found some local girls, and celebrated V-E Day with a ski meet.

10th Div. reacted to war's end by staging ski meet on Mt. Mangart in Julian Alps. The 87th alone had 403 killed during final months of hill warfare.

146

Endless maneuvers in U. S. gave way in 1945 to
fierce fighting in Italy. Most famous action was
night climb at Riva Ridge in the Apennines,

where 10th scrambled up rock walls to rout
the Germans. Above, first casualty comes down
from ridge on cable rigged up by ski engineers.

CHAPTER 13

SKIING'S WAR BABY

Fortunately, in the course of its training, the 10th Mountain Division made other forays to Aspen, all of them more successful than the Retreat from Red Mountain. On one of these expeditions, carried out in the summer of 1943, the 10th succeeded not only in advancing its own training — an entire company made the 164 miles from Camp Hale to Aspen and back — but also in planting an idea that would eventually flower into the most sophisticated and all-around best ski resort in the country.

In that particular company, there was an Austrian-born corporal named Friedl Pfeifer (see page 152) who not long before had been a resi-

Aspen combines good skiing, good living. At left, Francois de Gunzburg and Mrs. I. E. Peterson have lunch at sun deck atop Ajax Mountain. Above, Anne Chapman admires husband Ion's technique with Spanish wineskin; while, below, Anderl Molterer wins first World Professional Ski championship.

dent of the Bismarck, N. D., stockade where he had been confined as an enemy alien when the war began. However, unlike some of the other Austrians who were interned at the same time (and, incidentally, some of the yodeling Bavarians who are prospering in this country today on hastily renovated ideologies), Friedl was a genuine anti-Nazi. As such, he was quickly sprung; and just as quickly, he joined the 10th.

"When we came over the mountain that summer," he said, "we came out where the Dick Durrance house is now. And we washed our faces in the creek there before we came down. I'll never forget it because the country reminded me

continued

of St. Anton, if there is such a thing in America. We stayed three days and I got some time off and for two days I walked all over Ajax Mountain where the lifts are now, and I was tremendously impressed with it as a ski mountain. From then on through my whole army career at Camp Hale I came here every week end. And I got up before the city council and told them if I survived the war I would come back and try to develop this place as a ski resort."

This would take quite some developing. For at the time Friedl walked into town, Aspen was in only slightly better shape than Ketchum had been when Felix Schaffgotsch showed up. In the late 1800's Aspen had been a silver-mining boom-town. $10,000,000 a year in bullion had been shipped out on a rail line put in by the Denver and Rio Grande. Fifteen thousand people lived

there then, and they spent their money at the various bars, the three theatres, the race track, and the opera house that thrived in the bustling, cosmopolitan little city. Then, in 1893, the bottom went out of the silver market, and the people went out of Aspen. There were only about 600 when Friedl arrived. Of the mining, there was nothing left but a bunch of abandoned, rotting shafts that started on Aspen Mountain, ran five miles under the town, and came out across the valley on Red Mountain.

Surprisingly, however, there was evidence of a prior interest in skiing. "André Roche, who had been considered a ski-area expert in Switzerland, was brought here in 1936," said Friedl, "by Billy Fiske, the American 1932 Olympic bobsled champion, and some others to build an area the idea like Sun Valley. And Roche gave the opinion the skiing would be over in Ashcroft where it was all above timber line and no trail cutting to be done, where here the whole mountain was in timber. But he cut a trail on Ajax Mountain, anyway, because Aspen had bid for the national championships for 1941 and they didn't have a trail. The idea for the main skiing, though, was going to be on Mount Hayden in Ashcroft. But the war came and Billy Fiske was killed. He was the spark plug for the deal; and when he was killed the whole thing fell through.

"But I was convinced when I saw Aspen that this was the place, that we had to stay in the timber for protection against the wind and avalanches. I went to the Denver and Rio Grande Railway, and they showed some interest because of the defunct railhead they had coming in here. They furnished two lawyers to investigate the land situation, which they did while I was overseas."

While Friedl was overseas, too, Aspen came perilously close to losing its second spark plug. During the fighting near Belvedere in the Apennines in Italy, he had a lung shot out. But he made it back to a hospital in Palo Alto, Calif.,
continued

Early Aspenites brace for ride on cable-powered sled lift that ran up lower slopes of Ajax Mountain.

In 1941 D. R. C. Brown climbed Independence Pass. Today he is president of the Aspen Corporation.

where he filled the dragging months of his con-
valescence by browsing through some 400 defunct Aspen mining claims supplied him by the
railroad lawyers.

"Just before I got out of the hospital," said
Friedl, "I met over the telephone Walter Paepcke
from Chicago." Paepcke was very rich and very
bright. The son of a German immigrant, he had
founded the Container Corporation of America,
and built it into the country's biggest producer of
paperboard packaging materials. He had also
formed an idea that American businessmen spent
too much time getting rich and not enough time
getting together to discuss the true values of life.

"They should give more time to developing
culture in the country," said Paepcke, the evan-
gelist, "and," added Paepcke, the businessman,
"they should do it in a way to make culture commercially successful."

To achieve these apparently sympathetic ends,
Paepcke searched the West until he had found
first Aspen, and then Friedl. The town, tucked
away in an unspoiled Colorado valley, would be
a marvelous place to put on a summer cultural
program — music festival, philosophy seminars,
and all that. The man would help make culture
commercially successful by keeping the place
open in winter for skiers, thus providing the area
with a year-round income.

Out of this union of mind and body sprang, in
the fall of 1945, the Aspen Ski Corporation,
whose officers included Paepcke, Friedl, and the
inevitable Dartmouth skiers, Percy Rideout and
Dick Durrance, who had left Alta during the
war. (The Denver & Rio Grande gave up its ski
notions for good after a brief skirmish with
Paepcke.) Despite the power and passion of the
founders, the corporation remained for some
time a weak offspring. The cerebral types that
Paepcke sought stayed away from the summer
festival in droves, and those skiers who showed
up in winter were hugely dissatisfied.

"We opened up in the middle of December of
1946," said Friedl. "At the ski school that first
year there were four of us including me; we
grossed $3,000. We didn't have any trails ex-
cept the old Roche Run. Spar Gulch was skiable,
but barely. And we had no snow and the lift
didn't work half the time. The upper lift was
more or less a homemade job, an old mine tram,
and it was always breaking down and the chairs
jumping off the cable — awful. The only restau-

152

*Container tycoon Walter Paepcke planned summer-
time boom for Aspen, thought skiing was worth a
try since it might bring some off-season money.*

*Mountain man Friedl Pfeifer planned ski boom for
Aspen, thought Paepcke's money and summertime
customers could help bring year-round prosperity.*

rant in town, then, was an old saloon called Gallagher's that is now the Red Onion. The Jerome was the only hotel. It looked very discouraging that first four or five years. People would come to town and take one look and leave."

The first ray of light came from the summer operation. In 1949, Paepcke put on a show which, by all calculable indications, should have drawn only flies to a Colorado mining town: a 200th-anniversary celebration of the birth of Goethe. But, for some odd reason, attendance was good; people liked the festival, liked the town, and told their friends about it. With this injection of enthusiasm and money, Aspen struggled to its knees. It finally gained its feet after the winter of 1950. That season, the town put on the World Ski Championships. Through movies, and newspaper stories of the races, skiers learned that Ajax was as good as any ski mountain in the country. Through the grapevine, then only a faint whisper of the thriving network that today can make or break a million-dollar resort, they learned that the living in the town was both good, and cheap — $10 a week with breakfast at any ski bum's shack, and if you really liked the town, you could buy a lot for as low as $11.

"Nineteen fifty-one was the turning point," said Friedl, "from losing money to making money, where you could talk to somebody about buying Aspen Ski Corporation stock and you wouldn't get thrown out." Nowadays, the way to get thrown out of Aspen is to try to cut in on the corporation. For the town, both summer and winter, is a very fat operation indeed. To the cultural program have been added such noncerebral attractions as a golf course, dude ranches, and a glittering health center where physical therapist Tage Pedersen scolds, massages, and disciplines some two thousand people a year into a semblance of condition.

But the real source of money has been the skiing. Shrewdly and carefully, the corporation has plowed back its profits and pumped in new capital to build a total of six chair lifts and forty-one miles of beautiful, wide trails and slopes. The ski school, under Friedl and codirector Fred Iselin,
continued

Ski slopes undulate through variety of expert and intermediate terrain from peak of Ajax Mountain at 11,300 feet to edge of town where altitude is 7900.

Sally Kingman, of New York, left job to visit Aspen.

King of ski bums, Ralph Jackson, was ski instructor.

who came over from Switzerland in 1947, now grosses $200,000 a year all by itself. But Fred and Friedl, unhappy with the tiny trickle of beginners (throughout the 1950's Aspen's big play came from advanced and expert skiers), sold out their interests in the ski school to Aspen Corporation president D. R. C. Brown, and opened up a whole new area for novices called Buttermilk Mountain just 2½ miles from town. Halfway between Aspen and Buttermilk, both in distance and degree of skiing difficulty, is Aspen Highlands, an independent operation which Buttermilk and the Aspen Corporation now wish would get lost, but which will doubtless one day be asked to unite with the other two.

As for the old mining town, it has become, as *Sports Illustrated* described it, the City of Lights for American skiers. The Hotel Jerome has been joined by 64 other hotels, motels, and chalets ranging in price and style from the Garret dormitory, where teen-agers bunk for $1.50 per night, to the new Aspen Inn, where the healthier emigrés from New York's jet set sip white wine in the lee of the heated pool. Fifteen restaurants with bars, and 11 without, serve everything from limp hot dogs to subtle European delicacies, with side orders of modern jazz and dancing till two in the morning. Up on Red Mountain, where Corporal Pfeifer once washed his soldier's sweating face in a brook, stands a collection of $100,000 chalets where such people as Peter Vought (as in Chance-Vought) appear at the more fashionable parties. The vacant building lots that sold for $11 apiece in 1951 went in 1962 at a price of $30,000 for seven of them; and an acre the Corporation bought for $25 in 1945 has been bid up to $76,000. In fact, even the ski bums now have an air of prosperity, the old-fashioned male snow shovelers and general handy men having given way to well-to-do college graduates—mostly girls—on a premarital fling.

For all the gloss, however, the town will probably survive its present tendency toward becoming a kind of Murray Hill with snow. For one thing, at the center of both the Corporation and the social structure of Aspen are the Pfeifers, the Durrances, the Iselins, D. R. C. Brown, and architect Fritz Benedict, who are outdoor people with a primary love of skiing, and sound ideas about the kind of town they want to live in. Second, the mountain is so good that no matter what else happens in town, the big winter attraction in Aspen will always be the skiing.

Above, dashing pro racer Anderl Molterer (left) pauses for a drink with a pair of friends. Below, Fred Iselin powers through fresh powder on Bell Mountain, a shoulder of Ajax. Because of timber cover which holds back avalanches, Bell is one of the safest of America's famous deep powder runs.

CHAPTER 14

A TIME OF CHANGE

The year 1950 was one of change — and not just for Aspen; it also marked the end of the old ways for all of U. S. skiing. Up to that time, an American resort was a cheerful but unprofitable experiment, and the customers were mainly college kids and a few rich people out for laughs.

From now on, it was going to be different. Skiing was going to make a major bid — and a successful one — for an important segment of the country's winter tourist trade. Locally, youngsters and grown-ups by the thousands would take it up as a delightful way to fill their leisure time. Along with the surge of interest would come an awesome amount of building, which would increase the number of recognizable ski areas from about 40 in 1950 to more than 200 by 1960. In the West, this change was led by Aspen, and by Sun Valley which about this time abandoned the cheerful philanthropy of writing off losses against the UP's publicity budget, and began luring real, live skiers to its ski lifts. In the East, the bell cows for the new era were the Mt. Mansfield Corporation at Stowe, Vt., shown on these pages, and her neighbor, Big Bromley, whose story is told on pages 162–163.

Stowe was built by two men (below), who arrived in town 10 years apart, and from opposite ends of the earth. The first to show was an Austrian named Sepp Ruschp, at that time a restless, ambitious young racer from the village of Linz. In 1936, just after he won the Austrian national cross-country title, Ruschp and some of his rac-

When C. V. Starr (below, left) met Sepp Ruschp, Stowe was a small, crowded ski area. Together they built it into the richest, best-run Eastern resort.

ing cronies were cornered by one of the czars of Austrian ski racing. "You boys with all your championships," said the man. "Why don't you get out and use your experience instead of racing until you die?" This seemed like a fair question to Sepp, who scraped up a list of 80 or 90 small ski clubs in the U. S. and wrote to each one of them, applying for a job as instructor. He got four replies, the most promising from Stowe.

When Sepp arrived in Stowe, his first impression was hardly favorable. There were no lifts anywhere. The CCC had cut three narrow trails — the Nose Dive, the Chin Clip, and the Bruce — that wandered through the state-owned forest on the east face of Mt. Mansfield. There were only four inns in the entire area catering to skiers. And the day Sepp arrived, Dec. 10, 1936, there was very little snow.

"This was like a lost territory," he recalled. "I looked around and I said to myself, 'O.K., I'm in America, but where is the skiing?'" A few days

continued

later he went looking. Climbing the mountain on a private toll road that ran from his quarters in the tollkeeper's cottage to the Mt. Mansfield Summit House, a summer inn that still sits at the top of the mountain, he took his first run in America. "I skied the Nose Dive in new powder snow," he continued, "and I saw this was not so bad. A little wider here, a little this, a little that. Later I looked to myself a map. I saw — my gosh — New York, ski trains, crowds. And I realized all you got to have is trails, tows, inns."

He set out to get all three. That first winter Sepp and the Mt. Mansfield Ski Club put up a rope tow on pasture land rented from the Mt. Mansfield Hotel Co., owners of the Summit House. The Sepp Ruschp Ski School, made up entirely of Sepp Ruschp, gave 1,100 lessons at one dollar apiece. The Lodge, a rustic inn about 300 yards from the tollhouse, took in about $6,000 from visiting skiers. Sepp himself netted about $1,100, plus a degree of ill will from some locals who did not care for the notion that a foreigner was making money by running skiers up and down the sacred face of Mt. Mansfield.

That summer Sepp went home to Austria, fetched himself a bride, Hermine, and came back to Stowe. In spite of the presence of a new wife, the winter was gloomy. Skiers were scarce, money was scarce, relations with some of the natives deteriorated and, to top it off, Sepp broke his leg in a spring race. By summer he was ready to abandon Stowe and take an offer from Yellowstone National Park, but the Mt. Mansfield Hotel Co. came to the rescue with a proposition that kept him in Stowe and, hence, probably saved the future of skiing in the Mt. Mansfield area. Under the new agreement, the hotel opened up another rope tow, widened the slope, built a small restaurant, and made Sepp for all practical purposes the manager of the Mt. Mansfield winter operation with a contract that awarded him 20 per cent of the profits. This was a little more like it.

The next fall, in 1939, the Lodge was bought for $35,000 by George Morell, of Morristown, N. J., and its guest capacity was doubled. Two new trails were cut. And a group of New Yorkers, headed by radio broadcaster Lowell Thomas, and Roland Palmedo, an investment banker who

In 1960 new Mt. Mansfield double chair supplemented old chair for which Starr waited 90 minutes.

158

had made some of the pioneer ski trips to Stowe, formed a company to build a chair lift, the Mt. Mansfield Lift, Inc., capitalized through the sale of stock to $90,000.

"I know," said Sepp. "I bought $400. Magnificent." The lift went up — 6,330 feet long, the biggest in the country at that time. A warming hut called the Octagon was built at the top. At the bottom the state put up a warming shelter and restaurant and cleared a parking lot.

The new lift opened on Nov. 17, 1940. "I remember that very clearly," said Sepp. "It was my birthday. The lift got stuck. There was 49 newspapermen dangling in the air for over an hour. Blinding snowstorm. We had to pull them down with ropes, like the *Wolga-schiffer.*"

In spite of this unhappy beginning, the new lift recorded 57,266 single rides during the winter of 1940–41. The ski school had grown to a strength of 10. The Toll House Inn, rebuilt as a ski lodge, did a gross business of $48,000; the rest of the development grew apace. That was the condition of Stowe when the war broke out; and it was still the condition of Stowe at the end of the war when there arrived in town the second half of the team that has pulled the resort to its present prosperity. The new arrival was a busiman as big as Harriman, five times as tough as Paepcke, and quieter than the winter snow. His name was Cornelius Van Der Starr, and he wanted a ski lesson from Sepp Ruschp.

Mr. Starr had come to Stowe over a long and winding path. The trail began, of all places, in Shanghai, where Starr stepped off the boat in 1919 as a mustered-out machine gunner from the AEF. Within three weeks he had taken over the small insurance department of a local bank, hired two low-priced Chinese clerks, moved into a couple of rooms at the corner of Nanking and Szechuan Roads, and put up a shingle: "American Asiatic Underwriters." As his first move, he acquired the Shanghai agencies of four American companies — Hartford, Fireman's Fund, Continental, Great American — and set about insuring everything from a boatload of Czech refugees to a touring baseball team that wanted to be protected against rain. Soon he was running an underwriters' pool that included such giants as U. S. Fidelity and Guaranty and National Union. Working with silent purpose, he knocked off his competitors not only by giving higher commissions and bigger rebates but also by hiring smart Asiatics in preference to mediocre Europeans, by giving his Chinese employees both his loyalty and his respect, and by paying off claims at full value instead of taking advantage of some favorable shift in the currency rates.

In 1926, Starr formed American International Underwriters (headquarters in New York). He arranged reinsurance deals with companies like Swiss Reinsurance, Sedgwick Collins in London. He moved into the Philippines, Southeast Asia; he bought a newspaper, cooked up some real estate deals. When the Japanese cut off his China operations, he turned to South America, prospered there, and picked up in Shanghai again as soon as the Japs went home. By the time he arrived in Stowe that week end in the winter of 1946, there was no one man in the entire insurance world who stood taller than C. V. Starr.

There was also no one in the line waiting to get on the chair lift who was more impatient. For this was a normal week end in Stowe; hence, Sepp and his wealthy pupil waited an hour and a half for a ride on the chair lift. Starr asked why the lack of uphill facilities. Sepp had a ready answer: lack of money. Starr had a ready solution: his money. After a decent interval he loaned Sepp $38,000. Sepp threw in $8,000 of his own, got another $34,000 from the local stockholders of the Mt. Mansfield Hotel Co. By the winter of 1947 there was a 3,000-foot T-bar lift, since lengthened to 4,000 feet, on Mt. Mansfield. There were also five separate companies running the business — the hotel company, the lift company, the T-bar company, the Lodge, and the ski school.

Such a chaotic arrangement sat poorly in the mind of C. V. Starr. Forthwith, he produced $75,000 and bought 3,500 acres of skiing ground — practically everything not owned by the state or by the hotel. He moved into the Mt. Mansfield Hotel Co., increasing its capitalization from $50,000 to $325,000 (majority stockholder: C. V. Starr). The hotel company then bought out the chair lift for $300,000; absorbed the ski school and the T-bar; and the whole was reincorporated as the Mt. Mansfield Co., Inc., Sepp Ruschp, Vice-Pres. and Gen. Mgr.

"So then," said Sepp, "we had everything under one company except the Lodge." That fell in November, 1950, for $250,000, and Stowe, like Aspen, had become a mature business ready for the final spurt that has made it the very model of a modern ski resort. The next year a 2,000-foot T-bar went up on Spruce Peak. The Toll

continued

House Inn was improved to the point where it could unblushingly charge $8–10 a night; a swimming pool, tennis court, and golf driving range were added to the Lodge for summer guests.

There was one more project that needed financing, a double chair lift complete with trails, restaurants, etc., on Spruce Peak. Cost: $750,000 plus another $250,000 for improvements in the entire area, a loan that C. V. Starr preferred not to float alone. To get the money, he and Sepp worked the final miracle in the conversion of Stowe. They got the Vermont banks, some owned by the original anti-ski New Englanders, to lend $500,000. Starr matched it.

That finished, for the time being, the construction of uphill facilities (another double chair has since been added on Mt. Mansfield), and Stowe settled back for a brief period of leveling off. In 1954, the first year the Spruce chair was working, the corporation's profits were handsome. From a gross income of $1,136,776.02 the Mt. Mansfield Co., Inc. took in a neat 6 per cent gross profit — and immediately plowed most of it back into improvements on the buildings and ski slopes.

That December, the 63-year-old Starr wound his legs through the rungs of a chair in the dining room of his Fifth Avenue apartment, ran a surgically clean hand over his jutting chin, and mused softly on his ski resort. Plainly he was pleased. "When we came to Stowe," he said, using the plural pronoun of business royalty, "there were five companies, all fighting each other. Now they're all together, purring like kittens. And," he added, "I believe we're the only big ski resort that makes money."

Stowe did, indeed, make money, and so did

Master stroke in improvement of Stowe was hiring of Czech maître d'hôtel Ivor Petrak. Above, Ivor gives sample of his superb food and service to Honoré Bonnet, manager of French ski team. Another important move was opening of Spruce Peak, where instructors, at right, are enjoying new powder.

Sepp Ruschp, who by this time was the president of the consolidated, thriving Mt. Mansfield Corporation. However, the money, handsome as it was to Sepp, or to you or me, was still small potatoes to C. V. Starr. By his own word, he owned or controlled "at least 100 companies in 100 countries. By reinsurance we guarantee over half of the Norwegian merchant fleet."

In this impressive setting, Stowe was really no more than a hobby and, at that, only one of several hobbies. Some of the others, all staunchly unpublicized, were the annual support by scholarship of 20 to 30 foreign students in U. S. colleges; investment in another ski development at St. Anton, Austria; and the underwriting, to the tune of $100,000, of a new Metropolitan Opera Company production of *Madame Butterfly* (Starr thought the old show was in poor taste).

"I am not seeking any publicity," Starr continued, "and I don't want any. I try to stay in the background, and I believe my manner is quiet." Starr's voice, as he said this, was indeed quiet and controlled. "I'm just an angel, a backer," he said. "Really, there is no difference in having a yacht, or a racing stable, or an actress, or a ski resort. It's no more expensive. But my business has very little to do with skiing." He gestured across the room to Sepp Ruschp. "Sometimes I find a man who has an inner fire — a man who is perfectly in his métier, his orbit. And when I do, I back him." He pointed to Ruschp again. "I picked you," he said softly, then turned to his listener, "and Sepp isn't the first. In my own business I've backed some of the greatest young insurance people. And—" the hand again sweeping the air — "I've never been wrong . . . so far."

This is Big Bromley, Vt., the ski resort that Fred built.

CHAPTER 15

THE SNOW FARMER

There are two ways to put together a successful ski area. One is the Stowe-Aspen-Sun Valley concept of a glittering vacation resort. The other, pioneered by Fred Pabst, Jr. (above, right), is the mass-production week-end area.

Either way, it has to be done with money. Pabst, the Blue Ribbon beer scion, had the money. He also had a monumental disinterest in

beer. But he did like farming, which he studied at the University of Wisconsin. More than that, he liked skiing, and traveled to Europe in pursuit of it. When he came back to America in 1934, he toured the entire northern part of the continent looking for a place to put a ski area of his own. He went to Alaska, Mt. Baker, Yosemite, Sun Valley, Aspen. "I even went to that place in Oregon — Mt. Hood. But the government owned all the land and I decided the government was a lot of red tape. They even offered me free WPA labor at Mt. Hood," said Pabst, who has a Midwest Republican's loathing for Big Government, "but I couldn't take the idea, so I headed east."

His eastward journey was an odyssey of acquisition and invention unmatched in the history of skiing. He bought or built the staggering total of 17 small areas: Iron Mountain and Holton, Mich.; Scotts and Wausau, Wis.; five places in Canada; a couple near Lake Placid; one in Plymouth, N. H.; one in East Dorset, Vt. Finally in 1939 he came to roost on Big Bromley, near Manchester,

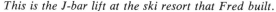

This is the J-bar lift at the ski resort that Fred built.

This is Fred — who had the right idea all along.

Vt. Along the way he invented a new high-capacity lift called the J-bar — a series of bent iron rods suspended at close intervals from a moving cable. Mechanically, the J-bar was a success, far safer and more comfortable than a rope tow, and infinitely more practical than a chair on the short-haul slopes that Pabst owned. Financially, however, his complex of small areas was a flop. "I was fifteen years ahead of my time," he said. "I had the hills, but where were the skiers?"

In most cases, the skiers were not as ready for Fred as Fred was for the skiers. One by one the areas folded, and he gradually began to concentrate on Bromley. But even that was a loser until, in 1947, Fred hit on another new idea: the way to get crowds was to make skiing easy. With this in mind, he proceeded to blast, dig, bulldoze and rake every rock, stump, and bump off the slopes. Then, reverting to his farm training, he planted the ground with oats or winter rye as a base, and with red top and timothy as topping. When he was through, every trail on Big Bromley was as smooth

as a baby's cheek. Whereas his competitors needed a minimum of one to ten feet of snow before they could open for the season, Pabst could operate with a mere four inches. And every flake that fell was rolled flat by snow tractors.

At the end of the 1949–50 season, the first in which the slopes were manicured, the number of customers rose from 10,000 a year to 35,000. Moreover, these were all-day skiers; they had to be. Fred sold no single rides. To keep the people happy all day, he instituted a baby-sitting service for skiing parents. He put in a fast-service lunch cafeteria, a ski shop, a protected sun deck. And he was smart enough to put them all in one building (above, left) at the base of the lifts and trails.

Today, the former Wisconsin agriculture student harvests a bumper crop of nearly 100,000 skiers a year on his carefully tended snowfields. And he is justifiably proud not only of the crop but of his original methods. "We farm snow," he says as the Sno-Cats rattle by on tractor treads, "and we have the same farm equipment to do it."

163

CHAPTER 16

OUT OF A MOLEHILL

Photographs by Pete Waldmeir

One of the most startling phenonema in the dizzy growth of skiing is a place in Michigan called Boyne Mountain, whose mountain (above), rising all of 485 feet, annually grosses some $750,000.

Boyne's healthy financial condition is no surprise to its owner, Everett Kircher (left), who insists that the measure of a good ski resort is not altitude. "If you took six Boyne Mountains and stacked them on top of each other," he says, "they'd equal Aspen. You can't ski all of Aspen on one run. So here you get the same effect, top to bottom, of making six stops out there."

Reassured by his own logic, he then goes on to compare the quality of his resort to that of his Michigan competitors, which, astonishing to say, number 85, more than any other state in the

Everett Kircher made a mountain of money out of a little Michigan hillock and a lot of smart promotion.

union. "We've got the Cadillac to sell and we're selling it," says Kircher.

The automobile analogy comes easily to Kircher, who, at 21, ran a couple of auto and trailer agencies before he bought the land to build Boyne. "I could see a helluva need for something in skiing that people could talk about," he says. "A big Shangri-La where they could get more than wet feet and cold noses." So he built one, keeping in mind three basic principles. Number one: "This business is built on sex, sex, sex. It's sex that brings the young men and women here." To make sure that nature keeps bringing them, Boyne is equipped with three bars of varying tone where singles of either gender have no trouble finding company. In the dining room of the main lodge, employees are instructed to try to seat single men and women next to each other. To run the ski school, Kircher hired, in 1953, Stein Eriksen. "Stein knew what they wanted; they

wanted him bareheaded in a bright sweater." (Later Eriksen moved on to Colorado, was replaced by handsome Othmar Schneider.)

Kircher's second tenet was to think big. He therefore poured $2,000,000 into his marvelous little mountain, which boasts five chair lifts, only one less than Aspen. The third principle was to make Boyne Mountain seem like fun: "Look. Everything smells like it was freshly baked. We can't let the customers know there is a cotton-pickin' hint of work involved in anything. Last night 3,000 dollars' worth of pipes froze up because some idiot was afraid to call me on the telephone. But this morning I'm around telling them it's nice to see them again. That's the challenge in this business: to do things on the sly. People don't like to hear your troubles. As far as they're concerned, I'm just a jerk who skis around all day and sits in the saloon at night having fun. I've got the role down to a science."

165

CHAPTER 17

RHAPSODY IN WHITE

Have you ever seen 10,000 skiers on a single hill? It is an appalling sight, especially when most of them are beginners. But it is a sight that, on any big week end, meets the eyes of the man at right, Walter Schoenknecht, impresario of Mt. Snow, Vermont. "We designed the area for volume handling," he says, matter-of-factly, "like a supermarket."

This supermarket philosophy infuriates some of his less affluent, more old-fashioned rivals who cling to the notion that skiing is a matter of the soul, and that five skiers on a slope is too many. "Go to Mt. Snow," says one, "and meet the Abominable Snowman." "See his Disneyland and Coney Island of the Snow Belt," says another. To these comments, Schoenknecht replies with a smile as cold as the tip of the mountain.

"When competitors hear my name they shudder, and I'm not surprised. History is in the making," he told *Sports Illustrated* writer Huston Horn, whose story is excerpted here, "for when it comes to developing a vacation spot second to none, Schoenknecht is second to none."

That history began on Oct. 2, 1949 — a date he is prepared to equate with Oct. 12, 1492 — when Walter Robert Schoenknecht (pronounced *Shawn*-connect) hopped a barbed-wire fence and half ran, half floundered to the summit of a snow-covered mountain in southern Vermont. "I stood at the top of that mountain — Mt. Pisgah they called her then — and I looked all around me," Schoenknecht said, richly savoring the moment. "I looked down at the snow at my feet — October snow eighteen inches deep. I looked out over that broad and beautiful valley falling away below me. And most of all I looked far off into the future. And there, just waiting for me, I saw the ski resort of my dreams: it would be the largest in the world, it would be second to none, it would be absolutely fabulous."

Nowadays, when Walt Schoenknecht ascends to the summit of Mt. Pisgah, which, with the blessing of a Madison Avenue friend, he renamed

Mt. Snow, he rides a quarter-million-dollar double chair lift ("one of the longest in the world"), and what unfolds below him is no vision of tomorrow. It is, rather, a pulsing, throbbing commercial empire which is, by count of customers, the largest ski resort in the world.

"In the ski business, I admire myself above all others," says Schoenknecht heartily. "I've got an uncanny knack for sensing what skiers want and the imagination and resolute drive to produce it."

By any interpretation, this is true. For while he has revolted the old guard by bringing the supermarket ski concept to its gaudiest flowering, he has also introduced legions of new people to the sport, and made them like it. He has catered primarily to the snow bunnies, those not-so-chic beginners for whom Fred Speier at Alta, with his beautiful mountains and beautiful powder snow, had such a deep yearning. Schoenknecht has given them a network of nine chair lifts, one of which rises all of 50 feet. ("A person can tell people he rode the chair on his first day.") His trails are wide and smooth and easy, so that a beginner can also brag, early in the game, that he has been down from the top of the mountain. Along with the lifts and trails, Schoenknecht has been smart enough to give his bunnies the extras most other Eastern resort operators deny them: a heated indoor ice rink, blocklong cafeterias, walk-in fireplaces, the first heated outdoor pool in the East (a big attraction, says Schoenknecht, "crowd-drawing-wise"), a resort-wear shop with a $100,000 inventory, dog-sled rides, dances, cheese-fondue parties on Wednesday, and church services on Sunday. "I also know," said Schoenknecht, "that a skier won't let you stand still, that you must provide something new, something tremendously exciting every year to get him back."

To that end, Schoenknecht peered into the future again and, with eyes watering, revealed to writer Horn his plan for expanding Mt. Snow to almost three times its present size, to a kingdom

Despite boos from traditionalists, Walter Schoenknecht keeps expanding at Mt. Snow, world's busiest ski center.

that will flourish both summer and winter. "We'll have a new motel," he rhapsodized, "that'll be really weird. It will have a trampoline in the lobby next to a 140-degree bath with a little Japanese girl scrubbing people's backs. Soon as we get that going, we'll start on a twelve-story hotel next door. *That* will have a bowling alley in the basement, an eight-foot flame and water-fall in the lobby, a real mountain stream running through the middle of the dining room, and a tropical garden in the corner." Summer guests may step outside to a 13-acre lake Schoenknecht made in the summer of 1960. There, they may

take their pick of a Passion play ("on a par with Oberammergau and box office second to none"), a symphony orchestra, Bavarian tea dances, or a ballet company. Or, perhaps, they may choose a turn on water skis drawn around the lake by an overhead trolley. Surmounting all will be a 350-foot-high fountain which in winter will build it-self into a 350-foot icicle. "You can believe it or not," says Schoenknecht. "Of course, these are merely representative of my ideas, some others of which are a little screwball. And of course we'll be careful as we go to avoid the Miami Beach look. I really detest Miami Beach."

167

CHAPTER 18

SUGAR AND SPICE:
(Notes on a Weekend)

While some resorts openly built for mass, others, most notably Sugarbush, Vt., aimed for what might be called class, and quietly hoped the masses — at least enough of the masses to produce a profit — might follow. Everything about Sugarbush has a special style, from the brightly colored cars on the Italian-designed gondola lift, shown at right, to the Manhattan jet-set clientele that swept in when the resort opened in 1958, to the scribbles under the phone just outside the men's room: instead of the usual information about Gloria, one scribble said "Fight Mental Health." For skiers who live in New York, there is even a special way to get to Sugarbush. This mode of travel — along with some other things uniquely Sugarbush — is described below in notes made by the author in the course of a week end.

THE BUS: Like anything else connected with Sugarbush, the chalet bus, coyly nicknamed the McIlbus or Sugarbus, has little overtones of chic which make the occasional OUTs who ride the bus feel OUTer, and the INs, INner. The bus is chartered from Greyhound every week end from New Year's Day to the end of good skiing, by East Side architect Alexander (Sandy) McIlvaine. It loads up in midtown Manhattan every Friday at 5 P.M., and McIlvaine, who also has his architectural paw in numerous Sugarbush houses, charges $15 ($25 round trip), plus $1.50 for what is called the lunch. This is really supper, a large bag of sandwiches washed down with white wine and preceded by a crude cocktail if one is smart enough to have brought a bottle, or smarter enough to have convinced a bottle owner to share. The various goodies are served by two stewardesses — society types like Marina Johnson and Marcia Breen—who get a free ride, or a cutrate ride, in return for chores. The bus driver is a

very attractive whitehaired man named Johnny MacBride, who, I understand, does TV and fashion modeling when he is not driving the bus.

The last time I rode up, a strict no-flirting-with-Johnny-while-bus-is-in-motion rule was reiterated for the benefit of one of the stewardesses who was getting bored with the trip, which took about six hours despite the fact that MacBride pulled over at one point to remove the governor on the throttle. On this same ride, I am happy to say there was very little group singing. There was, however, much congregating in the aisle of the bus, drink in hand, and a fair amount of seat-hopping. The fraternizing continued, at a rising decibel rate, for the entire 240 miles. I was surprised by so much jolly chatter. A great many of the passengers are repeaters, and I had thought they would give it the old Oyster Bay, "Hi, how *are* you? God, wonderful to see you," and then lapse into a six-hour coma. Not at all. The single ladies, of whom there are always several, do some vigorous spadework on the journey, as insurance against a lonely week end. And although a few of the males tend toward silence, they are basically party-oriented. The only professional travelers are the stewardesses and Sandy McIlvaine, who may at any moment swing themselves up into the baggage rack and snooze, solo, until the trip is over.

Once at Sugarbush the bus pulls into the parking lot (which is two degrees warmer than Mc-Murdo Sound) of the Sugarbush Inn, and the troops disperse. A fair number go on to Stowe or Mad River by taxi or in cars that usually won't start. My own experience was fairly typical. I

continued

Gay Estin, sister-in-law of late ski school director, leans from gondola. Turn page for more pictures.

Photographs by Hanson Carroll

was staying with the late Peter Estin, a postwar vintage Dartmouth racer, who, despite mountains of evidence to the contrary, swore he always went to bed at a quarter of ten. My own car, which had broken down in Sugarbush president Damon Gadd's driveway the week before, was supposed to be waiting in the parking lot. It wasn't. Therefore I tackled Sandy McIlvaine, who agreed to give me a lift. By the time I got my baggage to his car, every cubic inch was filled by utter strangers who had piled themselves and their impedimenta into Sandy's car, pleading for a ride to an inn called the Inferno. I picked up everything (the temperature this late March night was a certifiable 5 below zero) and galloped over to a Volkswagen which had been snowed in and had a dead battery. In return for promising to push it out of the parking lot, I was allowed to load my equipment aboard. My body could follow if the car started. So I pushed the car out of the lot and it started rolling down the road that winds up the long hill to the inn. It rolled and rolled, over a rise, around a corner, and out of sight. Fifteen minutes later (temp. still 5 below), it had not returned. Next move was into the Sugarbush Inn, there to buttonhole a friendly native who volunteered to drive me to Estin's. First we tooled down the road to find the Volkswagen, which was standing at the side of the road, lights out, engine dead as a smelt. After more transloading, we muddled along to Estin's. Twenty minutes later, McIlvaine, white with rage, stomped through Estin's door. McIlvaine understood I had a brown bag. Could he see it, please. I showed it to him. "Oh, God damn it!" Seems that of the six passengers he had taken to the Inferno five had decided they really weren't going there at all, and had demanded a ride back to Sugarbush Inn. Once there, they had piled out, bag and, apparently, everybody's baggage. McIlvaine had pur-

continued

Stockbroker A. Albert Sack, owner of a chalet in Sugarbush, snoozes in the sun while Melinda Weber basks in the lee of a reflector made of aluminum foil and old covers from Harper's Bazaar.

sued them, found nothing, and then by some odd process, concluded that it was I who had made off with his bag. Not having his suitcase, we offered instead a mild sedative (brandy), which he grumpily refused as he headed out once more on his frozen quest, followed by wife (now former wife) clad in galoshes and despair.

PARTYING AT SUGARBUSH: Next night there was a birthday party at Ski Club Ten for Igor ("Gigi") Cassini, who, until a recent bit of stickiness, wrote a regular society column under the pen name of Cholly Knickerbocker. Ski Club Ten is the heart of Sugarbush, a tastefully rustic building full of marvelous wines and equally marvelous girls, where *the* Sugarbush people go to feel distinct from the herd and to eat lunch. Usually, the place closes before supper as a favor to club member Armando Orsini, whose Sugarbush branch restaurant does all its business at night. But on this night Club Ten stayed open for Gigi.

I went with Estin, who swiftly vanished into the party, while I vanished into obscurity, finally fetching up against a plump, freckled, fortyish lady who felt about as relaxed in this swift company as I did. This was a costume party, a fact which most of the males had ignored but the women had not, a surprising majority of them appearing skirtless with black silk stockings and high heels that gave you lots of leg. The best of the legs belonged to Skeeter Werner, who has recently retired from international ski racing, and Faith McIlvaine, who had by now shed both her galoshes and her despair. The party ended when a fat stockbroker, who shall remain nameless, decided he was weary and must rest his eyes. That would have been all right, but the resting place he chose was in the frozen mud beneath his Jaguar, where he lay, feet protruding into the dark road. Harcourt (Bill) Amory decided that he should make his way out and rescue his good old friend the stockbroker, a charity to which the good old friend responded by leaping up and punching Bill in the face. This made everyone feel fairly morose, and they went home.

SKIING AT SUGARBUSH: The day after the party I went up the mountain with Peter Estin

Adorned with fur hat and racing number, model Cindy Hollingsworth enters Sugarbush slalom race.

and his mountain class. This is a regular crew of Club Ten people who used to take a long lesson with Peter on Saturdays and Sundays. They are a very El Morocco-looking lot, cool, but among themselves very jolly, quite good-looking, extremely sophisticated, foreign or quasi-foreign in accent, and all very good skiers. The group included the Count Vittorio Camerana and his wife Christine, Armando Orsini, Peter Estin, and one or two svelte camp followers. Also in the group was a stocky, lank-haired young man who smoked a cigar rather awkwardly and chattered in French and Italian as we rode up in the gondola. We skied the lift line fairly fast, and the young man kept bubbling in various Mediterranean tongues as he flashed in and out of the moguls on the hard-packed slope. "Ah," I said to myself, "a friend of Orsini's from Italy." Halfway down the lift line, we made a left onto a hairy trail that winds along through a lot of birch trees. The snow was deep, cut up, and a little crusty. The young man still skied fast, but not now so steadily. I stopped at the first turn and looked back just as he spun in a cloud of snow. He arose, smiled, said something in French, and came down another 20 yards. Suddenly he went down again in another cloud of snow. This time, he arose silently, staggered on another few feet, and almost fell again. The next word he spoke was pure Anglo-Saxon, delivered with pure New York inflection, and that was the end of the Romance languages for that afternoon.

When the young man was reorganized, we set out after the main body of the expedition. It was just around the next turn, observing the top of a small aspen whose trunk had suffered some recent bark peeling. Clinging to the top of the aspen, bending it with his weight, was a porcupine. Vittorio began tugging at the tree, apparently to get the porky close enough to grab. Christine slid over toward me. "How do you call that — that anneemuhl?" "A porcupine," said I. "Ah," said she, *"un porc-épic."* *"Oui,"* said I, *"un porc-épic."* "Oh," said she, "it would make a *di*-vine hat." At this point I persuaded Vittorio not to reach for the porky, and thus to save himself a swat from the prickly tail. Vittorio contented himself with shaking it down into the snow. Once on the snow, the porky soon set off into the woods with a marvelous, rolling gait. "Aha," said Orsini, "he has a good backside, I think, for merengue —" and with that the mountain class swept off through the trees once more.

CHAPTER 19

MAN ON THE MOON

Fifteen years ago, when this picture was made of Squaw Valley, Calif., no one but an idiot would have predicted that this would be the site of the most magnificent show in winter sports history. The valley itself is a marshy meadow near the pass where the Donner party, a pioneer caravan snowbound in one of the Sierra Nevada's appalling blizzards, turned to cannibalism. Only one person saw any future in the place: Wayne Poul-

sen, a Pan American pilot who wanted to create a tasteful little Alpine community where mountain lovers could come and love the mountains. To that end, Poulsen bought up most of the land on the valley floor (the U. S. Forest Service owned the mountains). Then he sought some new money to build his quiet paradise.

The money arrived in 1946 in the person of Alexander Cochrane Cushing (left), a sardonic Groton-Harvard product, whose purpose was to do something a little livelier than practice law in Wall Street. But the money almost was lost when Cushing had a conference with his equally sardonic wife, the former Justine Cutting of Manhattan, Southampton, etc.

"How would you like to live in these mountains?" Alec asked.

"Cushing," replied his wife, "are you out of your mind?"

By 1948, however, Alec had worn down the skeptical Justine. The money — $400,000 from Cushing and such of his friends as Laurance

Rockefeller and Jock McLean — was joined with Poulsen's land (640 acres) to form the Squaw Valley Development Corp. Out of this union came fame, fortune, and an aroma rather like that of an abbatoir.

It soon became apparent that majority stockholder Cushing and corporation president Poulsen were planning two different kinds of development. It also was apparent that someone would have to go. Before the first customer had climbed onto the big, new double chair lift strung up Squaw Peak, Poulsen's wife initiated a stockholders' meeting to get Cushing out of the corporation. But since Alec & friends controlled 98 per cent of the stock, it was Wayne Poulsen who went — though not all the way out of the valley. He still held nearly all the good real estate, which he had thoughtfully kept out of the corporation. The corporation, however, was sitting on six acres at the head of the valley, where the best ski runs ended and where the Forest Service had granted the exclusive lift permits for the valley. Thus
continued

Above main lift up Squaw Peak, Cushing installed 12-man tram which has won no prizes for design.

Cushing held home plate, Poulsen the infield.

With this messy line-up, Squaw Valley opened to the public on Thanksgiving Day, 1949. The opening was every bit as distinguished as the preliminaries. When the first guests arrived, the floor in the lodge was not wholly laid, china was stacked in crates outside. The domestic staff was so shorthanded that Justine pressed into chambermaid service an old friend who was sitting out her Reno divorce. Confusion swiftly mounted into disaster: somebody backed a car over one of Cushing's Lhasa terriers, a daughter broke her leg, and a seething line of people grew longer and longer outside the one functioning toilet. Through it all, Alec placated his guests with such soothing remarks as, "Madam, don't bother me."

The troubles of Squaw Valley did not at once abate — there were frequent floods on the poorly drained valley floor, frequent avalanches across the trails and lift line, and frequent battles between Cushing, Poulsen, and anyone who happened along to support or irritate either of the principals. It might have gone on like that forever, a tiny tempest in a remote Sierra teapot. But, in a whimsical moment in 1954, Cushing announced that Squaw Valley would bid to become the site for the 1960 Olympic Games. "I had no more interest in getting the Games than the man in the moon," he told a *Time* Magazine reporter later. "It was just a way of getting some newspaper space."

To Alec's astonishment, half of California (a half which did not include Wayne Poulsen) rose with a roar of approval. The state legislature said it was with him for $1,000,000 of public financing if he got the Games. And Governor Goodwin Knight said The-great-State-of-California-and-so-forth-and-maybe-there-would-be-more-where-that-came-from.

With that kind of money in hand, and the bit suddenly in his teeth, Cushing persuaded the U. S.

continued

French mountain guide Joe Marillac (above) arrived in 1949 to head up Squaw Valley ski school, is still there. Original lodge is not; it burned in 1956 despite firefighting efforts of Alec (right) and others.

When Alec first brought Olympic officials Wendall Broomhall and Donna Fox (right) to valley, Fox called it "low-class picnic area." Nevertheless, Alec won Olympic bid and hero status (below).

Olympic Committee to make Squaw Valley the official American candidate for the Games. Then he headed for Paris to take on the competing European resorts in the final bidding before the shrewd old gentlemen of the International Olympic Committee. In Paris, he was aided by two adroit, multilingual friends named George Weller and Marshall Haseltine who helped with contacts and urged Alec to make a soft sell, i.e, present Squaw Valley not as an embryo that would bloom into a great and glittering resort, but rather as a simple mountain retreat where the True Values of the Olympics would be reborn. Another aid to the Cushing campaign was a $3,000 12-by-6-foot model of the valley flown to Paris for the occasion.

"We set that model up," Cushing explained, "in an embassy building four doors down from where the other resorts had their exhibits. The 15 minutes it took a delegate to walk to see our model gave us time alone with him we'd never have gotten otherwise. Without that model, we'd never have done it. Actually, too, it was the speech that did it." He meant his own final, humble presentation to the committee, in which he offered such phrases as, "We're all sportsmen here, not politicians."

"That's when I thought we were in," he said later. "When we arrived in Paris, all the people representing the European resorts thought they could afford to be nice to us. When they finally found out how strong we were, it was too late."

Too late, that is, for anything but a bitter shouting war on the climactic day of balloting.

"It was damned exciting," Cushing recalled. "They were yelling and stamping their feet, and over it all you could hear the Russians yelling 'Nyet! Nyet!' " Apparently, they didn't yell hard enough. On the second ballot, Squaw Valley became the official site for the 1960 Winter Olympics. Alec had won perhaps the greatest long shot in Olympic history, and he returned to the U. S. braced for a hero's welcome. At Lake Tahoe near Squaw Valley, he got it (left). But from another quarter — namely, that of solemn, powerful old Avery Brundage (right), chairman of the IOC — came quite a different reaction. "Cushing," roared Brundage, "you're going to set back the whole Olympic movement twenty-five years."

Avery Brundage, head of the International Olympic Committee, kept a brooding eye on Alec Cushing.

CHAPTER 20

FROM
MINUS TO
PLUS

To anyone sentenced by employment to do time in Squaw Valley between June, 1955, when Alec Cushing won the Olympic bid, and February, 1960, when the Olympics actually began, it often seemed that Avery Brundage's gloomy prophecy might come true. The footpackers above, trying without much success to stomp down a blizzard on the ladies' downhill course in 1959, were only one symbol of the valley's troubles. For the tempest of discontent continued to blow through Squaw Valley. But now the valley was no longer a teapot. It was an international sports arena, and the wind carried the odors of conflict to the capitals of Europe.

Naturally, the storm center at first was Alec

Cushing. Once he had recovered from Brundage's blast, Cushing sat down to try and figure out how on earth he was going to build the vast plant the Games would require. California's million dollars, which had felt so fat in his pocket on the way to Paris, was in reality just about enough to buy snow shovels. He had no real staff, no ice rink, no bobsled run, no dormitories, no press facilities; he had only one major ski lift, an inadequate lodge, some beautiful ski mountains (which, alas, were forever avalanching), and a huge commitment. He also had Wayne Poulsen, who was now triply furious because Cushing had conceived the Olympic bid without previous consultation, and had pressed ahead with it against

Poulsen's strong objections. A few of the minor problems resolved themselves – the old lodge burned down, to be replaced by a dazzling new one, and the IOC eliminated bobsledding from the 1960 Games. The big problems, however, lingered on, and by force of gravity kept attracting new ones.

Cushing's first move was to install himself as head of the Olympic Organizing Committee – not a bad idea from the point of view of the Squaw Valley Development Corp., which stood to inherit whatever Alec organized. He then talked a number of important California politicians and businessmen into acting as a watchdog commission to see that the program got going,

continued

and kept going. Somewhat to Alec's astonishment, that is precisely what the commission did. Cushing found himself replaced as president by a very tough customer named Prentis Hale, who was otherwise chairman of the board of Broadway Hale Store, a board member of the Bank of America, Union Oil, and practically everything else in California that makes money.

Just before Hale took over, a survey was made to find out exactly what Squaw Valley needed. The findings were staggering: they needed $8,-000,000 — maybe 10, maybe 12. The biggest chunk, $3,500,000, would go for an ice arena; $1,800,000 would be needed for a seven-building Olympic village. Sewage and water supply would be $720,000. Roads and parking, $450,-000; new lifts, $360,000. These were just some of the basics. The list went on and on.

As it went on, Cushing eased up to his successor on the Organizing Committee to offer a suggestion about the proposed plans. Prentis Hale had a counter suggestion for Alec: get lost. After a brief protest ("He treated me like a criminal.") Alec sized up the cold eye and strong right arm of Mr. Hale, and wisely got lost.

Subsequently Hale took on Poulsen, whose land was needed for parking and sewage disposal. Poulsen refused to grant the needed acreage. Hale said in that case California might have to condemn Poulsen's land and put things where they damn well ought to go.

So much for the boys in the back room, who were not heard from again seriously until the Games were over. Hale then turned to other matters. He leaned on the California legislature until the lawmakers handed over $7,900,000 to add to their original million. He grabbed a friend of Richard Nixon's and gave him a $25,000-a-year job on the committee. Everyone wondered why — except the man himself, Bob King, a pleasant sort who suffered no illusions about the world's values. "I'm not kidding myself," he said, "that the Organizing Committee took me because they like the way I part my hair. It was because I was working for Nixon and they thought I could get some more money." Not long after King got the job, the Congress of the United States voted Squaw Valley $4,000,000. "We're going after Congress again," said King, at the time. "We're asking another $400,000 for military support, and we will have another $2,000,000 worth of service equipment on loan."

That comprised the bulk of the cash financing. The Organizing Committee also got some high-priced help from big business: $500,000 worth of computers and personnel from IBM, $250,000 worth of timing devices and their keepers from Longine, and Walt Disney himself to handle the pageantry. "I spent a long time getting Disney for this thing," said Hale. "Open and closing ceremony — all that stuff. And it's all on the house — *on the house, for nothing.*"

While Hale, from his office in San Francisco, was whipping and cajoling the money boys into line, up in Squaw Valley a tight little corps was gathering to supervise construction of the Olympic facilities. The first to arrive was Willy Schaeffler, on leave from Denver University to be Director of Ski Events. Then there was Wendy Broomhall, a former U. S. Olympic official, who would lay out the cross-country courses at nearby

Olympic layout, ready in skeletal form for its trial run in the 1959 North American Games, included: (1) ice arena, (2) speed skating rink, (3) spectator centers, (4) hockey and practice rinks, (5) administration buildings, (6) press building, (7) Squaw Valley lodge, (8) reception center, (9) Olympic village complete with dining hall and recreation rooms, (10) 80- and 60-meter jumps, (11) Little Papoose chair lift, (12) ladies' giant slalom course, (13) ladies' special slalom, (14) KT-22 Poma lift, (15) ladies' downhill, (16) men's special slalom, (17) KT-22 chair lift built by Cushing under heavy pressure from Prentis Hale, (18) men's giant slalom, (19) men's downhill, (20) original Squaw Peak chair lift, (21) Squaw Peak tram, (22) Squaw Peak chair lift No. 2.

McKinney Creek. From Sacramento there was bright, tireless Bill Kerth to put in the main ice arena and practice rinks. And from an obscure corner of the University of Southern California's track publicity department came H. D. Thoreau, who eventually took over as on-the-scene foreman for the whole Olympic operation — a troubleshooter for Hale and a placater of the men working on the mountains.

For a while there was almost as much troubleshooting and placating as there was construction. Hale quickly clashed with technical director Alan Bartholemy over the occasional need to put the crass business of raising money ahead of Olympic ideals. The upshot was the firing of Bartholemy, a job done by Hale with more abruptness than finesse. Both the act and the method aroused some passion in the breasts of Bartholemy's friends, notably Willy Schaeffler. Since Schaeffler was too valuable to fire, and was about as easy to push around as a wounded tiger, Hale decided it was a time for soothing. The soothing was done and the construction went on.

There were a few subsequent resignations by minor personnel. These had no effect on the actual building program, but they did have an unfortunate effect on the press. One national men's magazine said in its April, 1957, issue: "Nothing short of a miracle will keep the 1960 Winter Olympics from being the biggest foul-up in sports history." In Denver, an obscure skiing paper said a great deal more than that, carefully sending copies of one particularly damaging story to key Olympic officials in Europe. While this may have helped circulation a little, it did nothing for American prestige in Central and Eastern Europe, where the people understood skiing a great deal better than they understood freedom of the press.

Despite all these shrieks, moans, and catcalls, by late 1958 the Olympic plant was taking shape — to the satisfaction, even, of Avery Brundage. "With all that money," said Brundage, himself a construction millionaire, "I don't see how they can fail." They weren't about to fail; and to make sure they didn't, in mid-February of 1959, one year ahead of schedule, they subjected the valley and themselves to a trial by fire, a test run for the Olympics called the North American Games. Said Schaeffler, "I would hope that everything goes wrong during the North Americans. That way we learn, so we make the Olympics the best."

Someone must have heard Schaeffler. A week

continued

Tough-talking Prentis Hale took over Olympic Organizing Committee, raised money, hired and fired, was prime mover in getting impossible job done well.

183

Photographs by Joern Gerdts

before the North Americans, a typical Sierra blizzard dumped 63 inches of avalanche-prone powder. When the snow stopped, the wind started, piling up huge drifts and cornices as it howled around Squaw Peak and the neighboring Olympic hills of Papoose and KT-22. Then the rain came, two inches of cold winter drizzle that turned the beautiful powder to slush, and turned Squaw Valley's dirt roads into a series of meandering bogs and rivers where Army trucks, buses and bulldozers roared and snarled through the mess, while any civilian car without chains spun its wheels, rocked, and finally stuck. When the rain finally stopped, another four feet of snow fell.

One of the saddest men in town that week was the young Navy ensign whose Seabee unit was assigned to pack down the snow on Poulsen's meadow to make a parking lot. He started bravely enough, but with the rains his parking lot slowly turned to the consistency of warm vanilla ice cream; sawdust spread to absorb the moisture just floated away, and one gallant bulldozer operator went up to his waist in the goo as his machine majestically sank from sight beneath him. Another unhappy figure was the colonel in charge of the Army construction contingent, which on Feb. 8 unloaded from its buses and headed smartly toward its quarters. Unfortunately, the man who was supposed to prepare the offices for the Army had the mumps. The building was locked, no one had a key, and the colonel, after boosting a man through the window, found the offices bare of furniture. "It wouldn't have mattered if our man hadn't had the mumps," said Thoreau; "we wouldn't have been ready, anyway." This was certainly true of the valley — where most of the rooms in the Olympic village lacked chairs, tables, bureaus, and sometimes beds — but it was even more true up on the mountains, where the avalanche crews were fighting a desperate day-to-day battle to get the race courses open.

Early each morning, the muffled boom-bang of their 75-mm. and 105-mm. recoilless rifles sounded through the gloom as they tried to shoot down cornices and loose snowfields with artillery fire. Then there was the more remote and spo-

continued

Upper slopes of KT-22 were a nightmare of avalanches the week before the North Americans. But snow rangers and course packers still got runs ready.

184

radic thump of hand-thrown seismographic powder charges, carried to places the big guns could
not reach. At noon or later, the avalanche men
would come swinging down on their skis, soaking
wet, exhausted. And as the week wore on, each
time they came down, another trail, another
slope, and finally another mountain was declared
unsafe. Anything they left open was doggedly
footpacked by struggling Army volunteers. A
couple of days before the North Americans were
to start, Prentis Hale said gloomily, "I guess we
prayed too hard for things to go wrong."

Then, astonishingly, things began to go right.
The snow eased off. Schaeffler, the irascible perfectionist who had been trying to run every one
of his ski races exactly as scheduled, gave in and
put all the Alpine events but the ladies' giant
slalom on KT-22, which the avalanche men were
getting under control. The Finnish cross-country
skiers poled their way around the courses and
emerged from the woods grunting "Hyva, hyva,"
which means a combination of "good, good" and
"go, go." Another Finn clocked a new world
1500-meter record on the speed skating rink, and
said, "You cannot break records on anything but
the best tracks." The Russians, Finns, Americans, and Norwegians hurled themselves off the
brand-new 60- and 80-meter jumps, and pronounced them superb.

The sun came out. It stayed out throughout
the entire 11 days of the North Americans which,
truth to tell, were not an aesthetic success, since
they were held on the fringes of a half-frozen
swamp that would stay a swamp until the roads
were paved the following fall. But the North
Americans were a resounding success as a test for
Squaw Valley as an Olympic layout, and for the
people who had done the building. There were, of
course, a few sour notes struck. Buddy Werner,
the best U. S. skier, eyed the courses and said,
"They've got a lot to learn here." They did, but,
according to the man who counted most, they had
learned enough. Friedl Wolfgang, the world's top-
ranking ski official, from whom a single word of
disapproval could have meant a large number of
agonizing changes, looked around Cushing and
Poulsen's old feuding ground and said, "What
I say about Squaw Valley is a big plus."

*Cross-country skiers practice at dawn on the meadow
by Squaw Creek. Actual cross-country races
were held at McKinney Creek, 12 miles away.*

187

CHAPTER 21

THE OLYMPICS

At the opening ceremony on Feb. 18, 1960, half the 15,000 onlookers were the men who had done the heroic building job. It had been snowing for several days, but as the ceremony started the sun broke out. At this, most of these tough, tired men just plain cried. Then the Olympic flame was lit, and the finest Winter Games ever got under way.

The first winner was Sweden's Sixten Jernberg (No. 43), who churned ahead to win 30-kilometer cross-country. Special jump (left) drew crowds of 28,000.

189

Helmut Recknagel of Germany won jump. Despite political differences, East and West Germany formed single team.

Another early winner, Heidi Biebl (left) skied strong, well-planned race to pick up the gold medal in ladies' downhill.

After six years as also-ran, Ernst Hinterseer, Austria, snaked through tight course to beat world's best in slalom.

As 11-day Olympics moved ahead,
22,000 people a day swarmed over
Squaw Valley, grabbed hot dogs
inside spectator center (left), then
climbed onto roof for better view.

It was a show worth watching.
740 athletes from 30 nations competed, among them Canada's pretty
Anne Heggtveit, who lost downhill
(right) but later won ladies' slalom.

Though weather stayed good
through most of Games, occasional
snow flurries brought out wild
and wooly (far left) assortment of
costumes among the spectators.

Some visitors came out of curiosity to see their first major ski
meet, others were lifelong ski fans
who shinnied up tall trees to get
glimpse of 80-meter special jump.

Though many racers claimed men's
downhill was too straight and
simple, others, like Germany's
Hans Peter Lanig (right), had their
troubles with bumpy upper slopes.

In ski racing, where contestants go off one at a time, part of drama is the clock watch. At left, American favorite Penny Pitou reacts to second hand which says that Germany's Heidi Biebl has beaten her.

Italian girls posted poor time, still managed to look both interested and sleek as rivals flashed down course. Like most modern racers, they wore light, tight clothing to cut wind resistance, crash helmets for safety.

Ebullient Finns gave victory boost to fine old cross-country star Viekko Hakulinen, who, at 35, had just finished superb anchor leg in cross-country relay.

U. S. had rough going. Before the Games, men's star Buddy Werner broke his leg; then came Pitou's loss, and stunning fall by Betsy Snite (below).

Switzerland, too, had its ups and downs. One of the downs was a perspiring Willi Forrer, who showed a reporter exactly where he made the wrong move.

But Switzerland had two strong ups, both in giant slalom. Most celebrated was men's victory by Robert Staub (below, left), the other by Yvonne Ruegg.

To close observer, most moving aspect of Olympics was faces of racers. Above, men's downhill winner Jean Vuarnet consoles weeping loser Adrien Duvillard.

Two weeks before Games, Norway's Haakon Brusveen (left) was reported doubtful starter. Here, tired and amazed, he learns he has won 15-km. cross-country.

To easy-going Roger Staub, everything was fun, nothing was amazing. After his giant-slalom gold medal, he was lifted above crowd (right) to smile and wave.

Betsy Snite saw five years of training and last hope for gold medal disappear when Ann Heggtveit won. But at end of race, Miss Snite bestowed a gracious kiss on smiling winner.

The moment he learned of his gold medal, Ernst Hinterseer (middle, left) said, "I quit racing." Then he posed for striking tableau with runners-up Hias Leitner, Charles Bozon.

Though she missed a victory, Penny Pitou won silver medals in downhill, giant slalom, also won plenty of laughs when she hammed it up for press with conqueror, Heidi Biebl.

Pitou, Biebl, and Traudl Hecher of Austria stand before Olympic flame with silver, gold, bronze medals.

Needed: New Games for Squaw

When the great spectacle of the Olympics ended with a massed choir singing Beethoven's "Hymn to Joy," the state of California looked around the valley and concluded that the only joy might be in the memory. There sat the Olympic plant, $15,000,000 worth, most of it owned by the state. But no one was sure what to do with it. Cushing knew what he was going to do with his part — the lodge plus the Squaw Peak lift No. 1, the Tram, KT-22 chair, and KT-22 Poma. He was going to make money. Poulsen had already made money, tons of it, by selling off parcels of his land in homesites. But the bulk of the facilities just lay there in the melting snow like a stranded whale.

One state official, Will Rogers, Jr., had an immediate recommendation: "When you make a bad deal, admit it. Let's get rid of Squaw Valley." Instead, the state did about the only thing it could have done. It retained ownership, but leased out its lifts, Squaw No. 2 and Papoose, to Cushing. Then a real estate developer named Bill Newsom got a 27-year, 10-month lease on the ice arena, the Olympic village with its 900 beds, and a scattering of other buildings. Newsom immediately put in $150,000 for improvements. Since then he has added more. To everyone's astonishment, he has also added a unique element to Squaw Valley: an ability to work with Cushing. "We're getting along famously," said Newsom. "He gives us a discount on lifts and ski schools. He realizes the people in the village are an asset to his lifts, and as for us, the lifts are the reason we are in business."

To keep business moving, Newsom promotes bus tours from Sacramento and San Francisco, encourages hockey tournaments and public-school ice-skating programs, has hustled up some summer business, including one 6,000-man convention of the Radio Church of God. During the first year following the Olympics, Squaw Valley had 1,408,-757 visitors. And in one winter week end in 1962, 36,000 people swarmed into the valley. What did they do? "Not a thing," said Cushing's manager, John Buchman. "Some of them walk around, or they may buy a beer."

To any veteran of the Olympics who had witnessed the heroic building job or seen the flashing skill and wonderful faces of the Olympians, the sight of the Squaw Valley tourists staggering around in their limp, wet department-store parkas and upturned boots was painful. But though this attitude was perhaps understandable, it was also ridiculous. Tourists are people; and, besides, the valley needs them if it is ever to get on a paying basis. The one major offender in Squaw Valley's post-Olympic life was not Newsom, or the tourists, or Cushing, or Poulsen. Oddly, it was the United States government.

The Olympics, besides being an athletic success, were an important diplomatic success. Irresponsible journalism had led Europeans to think Squaw Valley would be a supreme example of crass, commercial, ugly Americanism. Instead, they found a Games which everyone — Russians, Germans, Italians, French, Japanese — agreed were put on with grace, dignity, and a primary regard for sport. The Europeans were deeply impressed, but it was an impression that this country permitted to lapse. It should be revived.

The State Department, under its People to People program, should get together with U. S. and European ski officials to set up a perpetual series of Squaw Valley winter games. In fact, there could easily be a regular American competitive circuit — as there is now in Europe where the governments underwrite some of the costs — beginning with two Alpine meets in New England, a Nordic meet in the Midwest, two more combined meets in the Rockies, and then a climactic games in Squaw Valley. The costs would be comparatively low, the benefits high to spectators, competitors, resorts, and — old-fashioned as the idea may be — to the nation.

Photograph by Neil Rafferty

CHAPTER 22

LOOK OF THE FUTURE

The Squaw Valley Olympics touched off the truly modern phase in the growth of U. S. skiing. During January and February, 1960, it was almost impossible to pick up a newspaper or news magazine without reading something about the Games. Perhaps more important, CBS took its television cameras to Squaw Valley, and for the first time showed live skiing on nationwide TV. As a result, when the Games were over, there were very few Americans who had not worked up at least a mild curiosity about skiing. And, as evidenced by the week-end hordes that poured into Squaw Valley immediately after the Games, there were hundreds of thousands, perhaps millions, of new people ready to try the sport for the first time.

Happily, there is almost no end to the number or the beauty of the mountains in the U. S. where skiing can be developed. The Tetons (above),

continued

Crossing close to the top of a snowfield to minimize avalanche danger, Betty Woolsey leads two friends on the long traverse from Olympic Ridge over to the snow trails through North Woods.

Three thousand elk, of the Jackson Hole herd of some 11,000, gather near the foot of Snow King Mountain to fatten up on the hay provided for them at the Jackson Hole Wildlife Park.

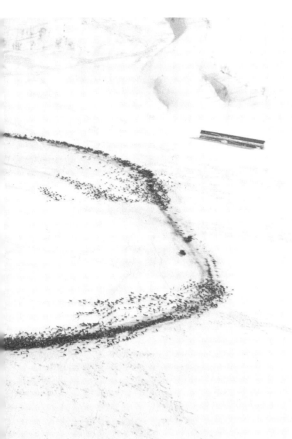

at Jackson Hole, Wyo., are only one example out of many, but a typical one in terms of assets and potential problems. Jackson Hole already has a chair lift up Snow King mountain right at the edge of town. Snow King is a good mountain, steep, well snowed, and well run — albeit on a modest scale — by general manager Neil Rafferty. At the other side of town, Betty Woolsey, a stockholder in the chair lift company, takes small parties on ski tours over the superb snowfields (left) just off the road at the crest of Teton Pass.

Before it can grow, however, Jackson Hole needs more money, better transportation facilities and, just perhaps, improved taste on the part of the hotel and real estate people. The money problem may be in the process of solution. About 15 miles from Snow King, publishing and TV investor Paul McCollister is busy trying to raise the millions needed to put in a major ski development. If this goes through and starts luring people, there will be no difficulty in getting more money for other new areas around Jackson, thus giving the Teton territory all the ski facilities it will ever need.

As for transportation, while the situation has certainly improved since the day the Wyoming highway department turned its frosty shoulder to Count Felix Schaffgotsch, Jackson Hole is still not what could be called an open city. The road over Teton Pass is plowed — but just barely. The other route, the Canyon Road, is better, but still no bargain; patches of black ice and nasty rock falls dot the highway all winter long. The Jackson airport is a wonderful place for eagles and stunt fliers, but no place for jets.

Finally, there is the question of taste. Jackson is right next to Yellowstone Park, and at the conjunction of several national forests. Once a tiny cow town (some of its sidewalks are still board), it now does a thriving summer business in automobile tourism. The neon-draped motels, hotels, bars, and souvenir shops built to accommodate the tourists have done very little for the tone of the place. Perhaps this doesn't matter to the summer trade. But as Aspen, Stowe, and Sun Valley have proved, to get the kind of people who will spend money to go to a distant resort for a ski vacation, the resort must maintain a certain style. Without that style, the only recourse is to play for the week-end crowds, which, in the case of Jackson Hole, is impossible; there is no big city within 200 miles to provide the crowds.

207

Photographs by Fred Lindholm

White Snow and Greenbacks

While the ski developers at Jackson Hole were out looking for money, a Colorado group called Vail Pass Associates was out getting it. Partly by borrowing, partly by selling general and limited partnerships in a proposed ski area 107 miles west of Denver, they picked up a fast $1,800,000, and then started building. When they opened on Dec. 1, 1962, they had a 9500-foot gondola lift with a chalet restaurant at the top, two double chairs, a Poma lift, and the nucleus of a plush village at the base of the mountain along Route 6. It was the most awesome start, in point of finance and construction, in the history of skiing. By 1965, the investment will have passed $10,000,000. It will be money well spent: the main trail down the front of the mountain is 2.7 miles long with a 3500-foot drop; the open terrain on the back side of the hill is as vast and varied as any in Europe; the highway will soon be four lane; and Vail will be among the top six U. S. ski resorts.

208

High peaks, huge bowls, and open slopes at Vail are reminiscent of finest Tyrolean resorts, while altitude (8,200 up to 11,250) assures long season of skiable snow. Painting below shows vastness of Vail enter- prise. Gondola lift rises from village at extreme left to Alpine meadow (left center). From there, double chair goes to top of timbered peak in center. A second double chair lift services the slopes on the right.

Switzerland
à la Pueblo

At one time or another every U. S. resort owner has claimed that he alone has established a ski area with the irresistible, European-style combination of quiet charm and bold mountain scenery. But until Ernie Blake (right) came along, nobody really had. Blake is a quick, good-humored Swiss who found an isolated snow bowl 9400 feet up in New Mexico's Sangre de Cristo mountains. The ski hill, rising sharply from the valley floor to 11,200 feet, was covered with a November–May blanket of powder snow as light and fluffy as Alta's. The nearest habitation was the Indian village of Arroyo Seco 10 miles down the Hondo Canyon on a mule track. Nine miles beyond that was the old Spanish town of Taos,

From his beginnings as a ski-train attendant 25 years ago, Ernie Blake has gone on to build a European-style resort in the mountains of New Mexico.

where a colony of artists had convinced every new merchant — including Safeway, Conoco, and J. C. Penney — to cut out the neon and build one-story adobe buildings. At one corner of the town was an authentic pueblo, founded in the 13th century and still full of Indians wearing blankets and high-crowned Spanish hats, horses, buffalo, and pigs, but no souvenir stands.

The over-all setting was perfect, and Blake did nothing to spoil it. At the base of the ski hill, he put up a cozy 20-bed inn run by two French skiers, Jean and Bernard Mayer, who know how wine and salad should taste. Near by, there are two dormitories, a ski shop, and a brand-new hotel owned by ski instructor Chilton Anderson. Above the valley, the trails are steep, the powder deep, the skiing marvelous (left, below). Because of its isolation and a studied lack of publicity-seeking, very few people have discovered Ernie Blake's valley. But the word is getting around, and despite the owner's mock despair ("In summer we live off the tax losses we suffer in winter"), Taos is fast becoming a money-making model of the small, successful ski area of the future.

Once or twice a season, Taos is invaded by Texans, whose skiing — and choice of costume — is fearless.

Jean and Bernard Mayer mix excellent drinks by night, teach in Blake's ski school by day.

One of hottest skiers in Taos is Lee Varos, Pueblo Indian whose ancestors settled region in 13th century.

Skiing
with a Smile

Photographs by Jim Rice

One recent morning a young man staggered out into skiers' dawn (9:15, when the lifts start running) and groped toward the new double chair at Big Mountain, Mont. As he arrived at the loading platform, the lift attendant held up his left arm and said something. The skier backed off hurriedly and said, "What's wrong?"

"I said, 'Good morning, sir,' " replied the smiling attendant. It took the skier the full 2200-foot vertical ride on the two-stage lift to digest this pleasant incident. But it was only the beginning. At the top of the mountain (above), he found scenery right out of an old Japanese ink drawing. On the way down the wide-open slopes, which hold a good depth of light snow despite a southern exposure, he fell in with the area's paid ski patrol, all good skiers and all friendly. ("Ex-

Snowstorms sweeping in from the West turn Big Mountain's trees into weird snow sculptures. Below, instructors make torchlight run on the lower slopes.

cuse me, but we have to close this trail for a while this morning.") In the Chalet at lunchtime was an easy-going crowd of young families, most of them from the Northwest. During the meal, three strangers asked if he was skiing alone, and would he care to join them? That night there was a dead-game beer and twist party at the Lodge, and when the man left, regretfully, three days later, a ski school instructor took the morning off to drive him, free of charge, to the airport.

It was all very natural, and in three years since the chair was built, it has made Big Mountain the pleasantest small, family resort in the U. S.

Big Business

The stern, imposing structure above is the Broadmoor Hotel, the heart of a $75,000,000 spa in Colorado Springs. Since 1931, when the Broadmoor remade its indoor polo field into a huge ice arena, the resort had turned a good dollar in winter. Then, in 1958, it decided to do even better. Steve Knowlton, a 10th Mountain Division veteran, was hired away from his night club in Aspen to set up a ski hill near the hotel. This Knowlton did, complete with double chair and artificial snow-making machinery — the latter is a necessity on the dry foothills of the eastern slope of the Rockies. To the Broadmoor's astonishment, most of its early skiers were not hotel customers, but local people who like to ski. Last year, some of the guests began to trickle out to the ski hill, and liked it. Other hotel groups, like the Homestead in West Virginia, and the Mt. San Jacinto Winter Park Authority in Palm Springs have recently put in ski lifts of their own. More will follow.

214

Big Brother

Two thousand miles from the Broadmoor, in both distance and concept, is the state-owned ski area on Whiteface Mountain, N. Y. The brainchild of then-governor Averill Harriman, Whiteface opened in 1958 to provide the people of Upper New York State with a winter playground. The opening of the Whiteface chair lift was remarkably like the opening of Harriman's pioneer chair at Sun Valley 22 years before. In the midst of the inaugural ride, the lift broke down. This time it was not the office help but Harriman (above) who dangled in the company of a wistful aide. After 30 minutes, they got Harriman down and the place running — to the dismay of some private operators. "Harriman wants to be remembered as the old White Face," said one lift-owner. "They've got millions in state money in there in competition with free enterprise. That's socialistic." It may be, but it also is awfully nice for the people, who otherwise would have no place to ski.

The Sierra Runneth Over

Just down the back of KT-22, one of Squaw Valley's Olympic hills, there is a brand-new area called Alpine Meadows (below). It was put next to Squaw for two reasons: (1) the terrain happened to be good, (2) there is an old law of skiing economics which says if a new resort is built next to a flourishing old one, then both places will get a double dividend of prosperity. For Alpine Meadows, the law proved out when they opened over the Christmas holidays in 1961. "We had 1500 people the third day," says general manager Tim Sullivan, "and we didn't even have the lodge or lunch service or even any plumbing. But we're not hurting Squaw, moneywise." Nor were they; the Olympic plant drew over 10,000 the same week end. Alpine Meadows was also careful to follow another economic precedent, this one set in 1939 by the nearby Sugar Bowl (right), oldest resort in the burgeoning Sierra complex. The founders of the Sugar Bowl sewed up all the land near the lifts, and parceled it out to corporation

In near future, Squaw Valley (above) may be linked with neighboring Alpine Meadows by chair lift.

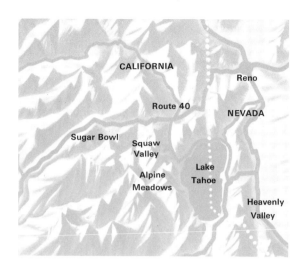

members for lodges — which have come to be used summer and winter. Alpine Meadows has taken this idea, added to it the Poulsen-Aspen gambit of leasing or selling not only within the corporation but also to high-bidding outsiders. Now, with three major resorts all within six miles of each other, and just across Lake Tahoe, Heavenly Valley (see map), with its brand-new cable car, the northern Sierra is bracing for a skiers' gold rush. "When Highway 40 is four-laned over Donner Summit," says Sullivan, "the entire Tahoe area will explode. Our problem is going to be to get ready to handle all the people who come."

Sugar Bowl (above), just west of Donner Summit, is oldest of four major resorts in the Lake Tahoe area.

Man with the Most Mountain

As the northern Sierra braced for its onslaught of skiers, an area in the southern Sierra 320 miles from Los Angeles neared the climax of a long, slow growth that may make it the biggest ski resort in California. The place is aptly named Mammoth Mountain, and its potential position at the top of California skiing puts it very close to the top in the future of all American resorts for a very basic reason: the state of California is now first in population in the U. S.

Obviously, then Mammoth will never lack for people. Nor does it lack for slopes; the picture at right shows only one relatively small segment of the 1000 acres of ski terrain. As for that other vital ingredient, snow, Mammoth, like the rest of the places in the Sierra, admits to a serious problem. In 1952, Mammoth had to close in April

because everything was buried, including the warming hut, which they managed to dig out in May. Ten years later, during a February blizzard that dumped 14 feet of 32-degree Sierra slush in one continuous fall, a reservations clerk told a long-distance caller, "No, you better not come. We'd love to see you, but the road's pretty bad and we haven't got the chair dug out yet." Thus the problem is a positive one of plowing the snow, rather than praying for it. The only limiting factor for this remarkable area has been the slow growth of its facilities.

Mammoth was started literally on a shoestring

by Dave McCoy (left), a Los Angeles County hydrographer. In 1938, McCoy put up a ⅜-inch thread of a temporary rope tow powered by the jacked-up wheels of his Chevy. In 1948, he made the rope permanent, and, in 1950, he put up a cozy hut nicknamed the Snake Pit by the jam-packed skiers who warmed it with the heat of their own bodies. It was six more years before McCoy scraped up the money for his first chair lift. But when the lift was finished, Mammoth quickly gained speed in its rise toward the big time. The next year another chair went in. Two seasons later, the Mammoth Mountain Inn went up, a $750,000 operation whose opening was a disaster even by the Sierra's high standards of opening-day disasters — a clever plumber had hooked the hot-water mains to the electric conduits. However, like its sister resorts farther to the north, Mammoth recovered from the debut, and swiftly grew into a mature ski area. Today it boasts no less than four double chairs, two T-bars, a million-dollar base chalet to match the expanded Mammoth Inn. Next season McCoy will add a 7300-foot 43-passenger aerial tram, and Mammoth Mountain will then be the number-one ski resort in the fast-rising number-one state.

PART III

THE ORGANIZATION

Held together — but just barely — by red tape, chewing gum, and not very much money, the official agencies of American skiing still manage to carry out their various functions, sometimes in an aura of confusion or despair, at other times with courage and distinction.

Somewhere between the middle and the bottom of the American ski complex, there is something that calls itself Organized Skiing. This title refers basically to the United States Ski Association, a largely volunteer organization which sanctions ski meets, appoints coaches and competitors for national and international races, holds conventions, elects committees and officers who argue with each other, but does little for the mass of recreational skiers. Because of this latter fact, most recreational skiers take almost no interest in The Organization. In the beginning, however, there was plenty of interest. There had to be.

When skiing first began in this country, there were no uphill facilities, no trails, and no one to ski with. One day in the late 1850's a bunch of California gold miners, tired of mushing through the Sierra all alone, got together to form a ski club. No one knows which miners or what club. But, anyway, they did it, and Organized Skiing in the U. S. was launched. It sank almost immediately, since this and subsequent Sierra clubs were fleeting things, pulled together mostly for laughs, or maybe for a single racing carnival. The Organization surfaced again in 1872 in Berlin Mills, N. H., when a bunch of Scandinavians formed a winter outing group which, with wonderful simplicity, they named the Ski Club (later renamed the Nansen Ski Club in honor of Norwegian arctic explorer Fridtjof Nansen). But the true chronology of a national skiing organization does not begin until two years later, with the founding of the Norden Club in Ishpeming, Mich.

By 1891, there were enough Midwestern clubs to band together in the Central Organization, which promptly languished from member disinterest. By the turn of the century it had shrunk to a few cronies who met evenings in the Trosvig brothers' chicken coop near Deer Lake. But on Feb. 21, 1904, Carl Tellefson of Ishpeming bravely convened these remnants, together with a couple of guys from Red Wing, Minn., in his office and said that what they needed was to call themselves the National Ski Association. So they did.

The next day, at a crude jump near the local golf club, they put on a meet, the first officially sanctioned competition by the permanent governing body of skiing. The NSA was under way. The longest jump at that first meet was 99½ feet by Julius Klustad of the Red Wing Club. For this achievement he received not only a handsome silver cup from the ladies of Ishpeming, but also (alarums, excursions, and portents) a cash prize. By 1917 the abundance of cash prizes had made professional jumping a fairly profitable avocation, as well as a source of irritation to those skiers who had joined clubs to jump for fun. A number of clubs dropped out of the NSA in protest; and although a great many more clubs dropped back in as skiing grew through the 1920's, organized skiing is still sharply divided as to how a competitor is to feed and train himself without falling into a cesspool of Evil Money.

Another of the Organization's problems has been to find its proper function. During the lift-building boom of the 1950's there was less of a practical need for ski clubs. If a person wanted company, he could find plenty. To ride a lift, he no longer needed to set up a rope tow. And, finally, it was no longer necessary to import a professional to get ski lessons, as the Mt. Mansfield Club did with Sepp Ruschp. The only real reason to have a ski club was just to be in a club, any club, and the only real reason for a national organization was, apparently, to handle racing. Since the average skier couldn't care less about racing, the clubs — of which there were, in 1962, 742 with 40,000 members — took less and less interest in the national organization. No interest equals no money. Total operating fund collected for the Association (recently renamed the United States Ski Association) in the '61–'62 season was $38,405. This modest sum paid the wages of the USSA's three permanent, salaried employees and helped take care of hundreds of minor expenses, such as Hall of Fame plaques. But it did not finance the kind of strong national organization which is now necessary.

Ski racing long ago ceased to be a jolly lark; it is a high-powered business, a type of international diplomacy, and a matter of national pride. Therefore, the selection and training of a team cannot be, as in the past, a matter of guesswork and improvisation by volunteer personnel. Moreover, a professional ski racing circuit has started, and a final, fair distinction must be made between pros and amateurs so the two can coexist. As for the recreational skier, though his basic needs have long since been taken care of, there are still some services the USSA can provide.

Some of these steps are now being taken. A $20 Participating Membership (i.e., no club affiliation) in the USSA provides, among other things, 2,000 dollars' worth of ski accident coverage. The USSA has recognized the Professional Ski Instructors of America, a powerful group of teachers who are four-square for establishing a standardized American ski technique, a gentle form of the shortswing, and may soon be able to enforce this technique on all ski lands leased from the U. S. Forest Service. The Pacific Northwest Ski Association is proposing a new type of divisional membership which, for $10, will give skiers discounts for lifts, ski shops, lodges, lessons, and restaurants. As for the more spectacular issues of racing, avalanche control, and snow safety, the organization's forward — and backward — steps are discussed at right and on the following pages.

At the lift terminal in Heavenly Valley, Calif., a patrolman straps in a casualty for ride down.

THE PATROL

There was a time not long ago when a skier who hurt himself in a fall was just plain out of luck. Such a luckless skier was C. Minot Dole, a New York insurance man who broke his leg while skiing Mt. Mansfield with his wife and two friends, the Frank Edsons, in 1936. While Dole lay in the snow, his wife and Mrs. Edson went to look for help. The help that returned was the two wives, with a piece of tin to hold his leg. Dole finally made it down the mountain; but nine weeks later, Frank Edson did not. Hurt in a more serious fall, Edson died. Dole started, then and there, to do something about snow safety. Within two years, he had set up and recruited the National Ski Patrol Service, with 94 volunteer national patrolmen, to help injured skiers, slow down *schuss*-boomers, and close off unsafe slopes. Today there are 400 local ski patrols with 5500 patrol men and women. All the skiers in the NSPS itself are still volunteers, but a few resorts now maintain their own professional patrolmen. Whatever the patrolmen receive for their efforts, it is not enough. They have helped to make skiing a safe sport.

CHAPTER 23

THE PREDATOR

Sometimes it starts with no sound at all. Across the top of a steep snowfield, just below the summit, suddenly there will be a crack that wiggles and darts and widens; and then the whole side of the mountain begins to move. At other times, when the air is cold and brittle after a long fall of powder, there will be a gentle whispering, almost a sigh, as the mountain shrugs to rid itself of thousands of tons of new snow. However it starts, an avalanche is a thing of terror. For there is no earthly way of stopping one until the rolling mass of snow — gathering strength until it roars like a freight train on a grade; gaining speed until the air blast ahead of it can knock a fleeing skier flat — decides it has run its course. Then the deadly snowfront stops of its own accord, leaving behind it a rumpled but cleanswept slash of hillside.

Men have tried to stop avalanches. High up they put snow fences, but these are swept away. Or, more ambitiously, they build avalanche barriers of great logs and rock. These are buried. The only way to combat an avalanche is to attack, to stalk the menace at its source. It must be treated like a predator, for in its lethal, lurking way, an avalanche is precisely that.

The business of stalking young avalanches is rough and dangerous; it takes rough men who are able to regard danger as an interesting companion. Such a man is Dick Reuter, six-foot four-inch, 212-pound ex-lumberman who came to Squaw Valley in 1955 to join the ski patrol, and found himself in avalanche country. "We skied 'em all off in those days," said Reuter as he sat

continued

Born in a gully high up in the Canadian Rockies, a deadly avalanche gathers power as it roars down.

222

We went as fast as we could. That way, if you was below the fracture line you'd have a better chance to ski out. One guy goes across; if he don't cut it off, then the other guy goes a few feet below him, and then the next guy. If that don't do it, then the first guy, he's it again.

"Sometimes you get a delay. I got one once. It cut loose — I was about 30–40 yards below the fracture line. It took me under. I don't know what it's like to be in the surf, but I imagine it's like that. I seen daylight a couple of times and then it was dark. That swimming to try and stay on top, kind of backstroking, that's just a theory. It could help if you get your poles off and your skies — that's why you ought to wear safety bindings so they'll come off and you got a better chance of swimming and fighting your way back up. That time I got caught I was fighting, but with those beartrap bindings it just wasn't no use. Well, finally that avalanche threw me out about 100 yards down, by lift tower 26. See, an avalanche has a rotating motion. It twists you around. That's why when they find a guy buried in a big slide, he's all twisted up. I was lucky. I got thrown out, and it was light snow so I didn't get beat up too bad. But if you get caught in one of those big, heavy slides, wet snow, those big hard chunks just grinding — boy, you've had it!

"Back then, skiing them off was our only technique. But at Alta, Monty Atwater was developing some better ideas. Monty came here in February of 1957. There was talk of an Olympics, and Monty came to get this place on the ball."

Eventually, Atwater did get Squaw Valley's avalanche control efforts on the ball, just as he had at Alta, where he was head of the U. S. Government's first and, for a long time, only avalanche research station. He started at Alta in 1946, the year after he was mustered out of the 10th Mountain Division; and he started with nothing, except the knowledge that he was the snow safety ranger in a place where the snow was not very safe. "We didn't have any defenses then," he said, "except a sign that said 'Closed,' meaning such-and-such a slope was closed because of avalanche danger." The signs were vastly unsatisfactory, since they neither prevented the avalanches from coming down, nor the people from skiing out across the forbidden slopes.

A slope that is ready to avalanche is often a slope that looks perfect for skiing — open, steep, and covered with a deep blanket of new snow.

continued

At 57 a tough and active 200-pounder, Monty Atwater pioneered avalanche control at U. S. resorts.

one night in the Squaw Valley Lodge, sweating out a Sierra blizzard. "Kind of dangerous business you could say. First thing after a storm in the morning, before we'd let the people on the hill, we'd go up and clear off the headwall. Where the slope starts to break over, we had a little tree over there we'd line up. We'd ski across, kind of pressing down on the skis, and try to cut it off.

224

Standing by recoilless rifle, Dick Stillman (left) and Atwater scan Squaw Peak for potential slides.

Linked together by the flimsy webbing on their ski poles, two patrolmen kick off the crest of a cornice.

As crew holds its ears against the blast, a rifle on KT-22 cuts loose at avalanche area on Squaw Peak.

Some people find the temptation irresistible, and, as a consequence, some people are never found. At first, Atwater tried skiing off the slides, to bring the snow safely down an empty hillside before recreational skiers were allowed on the slopes. But, like Reuter several years later, Atwater found himself taking some swift and nasty rides as one more piece of debris in the moving snow. There had to be a safer way than this. Atwater tried the first one in the winter of 1948–49: "The forest service had brought a lot of this demolition stuff, explosives, to Alta to use in trail building, and it was just lying around. They were hand charges, the kind with a fuse that you light. We knew the Europeans were using explosives, we just decided to copy them."

The first copies were not too precise. True, the shock of the explosion was often more effective than skiing an avalanche loose. Usually it was also safer than skiing, and always it was safer than another ancient but hair-raising technique known as "stomping," in which two patrolmen, roped together, pick their way along the crest of a high, unstable cornice, kicking off chunks of

snow that might otherwise crack off and start a slide when there is someone on the slope below. But the hand-charge method was far from perfect, the main troubles being that a hand charge must be either thrown (by a man wrapped to the ears in heavy clothes and teetering on his skis), or carried (in which case the avalanche often lets go from the vibration of the dynamite carrier's skis), or, ultimately, that there may be no human way to place the charge where it ought to be.

"We realized," said Atwater with a smile of weary recollection, "after we got piled up a few times using hand charges that there must be something better. So we began agitating for artillery, Army stuff, a gun that we could mount in a safe place and fire up onto the mountain slopes. The Swiss were using mortars. They still do. But you get too many muzzle bursts, and in the turbulent mountain air the projectile begins to tumble and you get duds. Besides it's hard to set the base plate; by the time you fire a few rounds, it's liable

226

to be six feet down in the snow.

"We finally got a gun in the winter of 1952. It was a World War I French 75 the Utah National Guard used to fire salutes down by the state capitol. That worked pretty good. We could shoot where we wanted without having to go up.

"We used the 75 until 1955, when the barrel cracked. Then we got a 75-millimeter pack howitzer, which is still in use in Alta. They keep it because they can fire it out the garage door. When you get four feet of new snow, you can't drag it around, so we developed this thing of opening the garage door and letting fly. Meanwhile, during the Korean War, the Army developed the recoilless rifle — only 167 pounds for a 75-mm. gun on a .30-caliber machine-gun tripod. It fires accurately to 2200 yards, and it's effective to 7000. We began agitating as soon as we heard about it. We asked every year, but we didn't get one till the Olympics got started in 1957."

With the Olympic planning started, and the recoilless rifle in hand, Atwater moved to Squaw Valley, leaving the Alta station in the cool and capable hands of snow ranger Ed LaChapelle. At Squaw, Atwater teamed up with an old avalanche-hunting crony named Dick Stillman to develop a snow-safety program second to none. By the time the Games started, they had a total of ten 75- and 105-mm. rifles and a corps of ten elite skiers drilled as snow rangers. Thanks to their efforts, there was not one avalanche casualty during the entire period of preparation for the Olympics, despite the hundreds and hundreds of men who had to work the slopes in all weather to get the facilities ready for competition.

After the Games, Stillman left to take over Berthoud Pass, Colo. But Dick Reuter stayed on and worked with Atwater, who began to further refine the methods of avalanche research and weaponry. "Come down to my witch's lair and see what we've got," Atwater said, leading the way out into the Sierra snowfall and down to the basement of what had been the IBM score-computing center during the Olympics. The witch's lair was a wild clutter of equipment. Ranged along the wall were a delicate wind gauge (37-mile-an-hour gusts on Squaw Peak), a precipitation gauge (4.4 inches of snow in one fantastic hour from 8 to 9 o'clock that morning in Siberia Bowl), and a temperature gauge (26° in Siberia, 22° on Squaw Peak, 33° in the valley). Atwater sighed, for the figures on the gauges added up to

At the top of a cornice, a hand charge of seismographic powder bursts in a shower of crusty snow.

the worst sort of avalanche potential. Tomorrow the battle would have to begin early, and he glanced at the weapons spilled around on the floor: two spare 75-mm. recoilless rifles; three portable radios in canvas bags; a pair of 7′ 3″ Head skis, coffin-shaped orange boxes full of

continued

Photographs by Fred Lindholm

At Alta, Ed LaChapelle (above, center), starts to ski through avalanche area. To his left, snow cracks.

Now the whole slope has let go; LaChapelle is caught. A tiny dot below the trees, he tries to fight clear.

nylon rope to be used by the patrol when they worked around cliffs or cornices; long, thin steel antennas taken from Army tanks, to be used as probes if the deep snow needed to be searched for bodies; five orange-painted shovels; an aerial photograph of Squaw Valley with the avalanches marked in colored grease pencil. Off in one corner was Atwater's proudest possession, a light, angular steel contraption. "That's my avalauncher," he said happily. "Some guy wrote and showed me one of those compressed-air pitching machines and said why don't you use this on avalanches. I asked the manufacturer if he could make it to throw explosives, and he built me a pilot model. It's going to be a wonder. It throws a charge about 400 yards; it fills a gap in our armament between the rifles and the hand charges which we still use in some places. The most advanced project is the rockets. They'll fill the gap, too, and maybe substitute a little for the rifles, which we have to fire blind and re-aim after each shot, and, anyway, they're so violent at the point of discharge that they tear down any structure near by — blow the windows out of the lift terminals. We tested the Mighty Mouse air-to-air rocket, but it was unsuitable. We're trying another rocket now. They're kind of wild. To start avalanches, we don't have to have absolute pinpoint accuracy, so long as we get within 50 feet of the bull's-eye. But we can't be firing all over the countryside. There are too many friendly troops around."

With that, Atwater squinted at his avalanche

228

map, gave the wind gauge an inquisitive tap, then turned off the light and mounted the stairs. "We'll be out tomorrow," he said, walking off toward the lodge. "You'll hear us in the morning." And that next morning a visitor to Squaw Valley having a late breakfast could hear the distant boom of the avalanche guns high on the peak, and be thankful for men like Monty Atwater and Dick Reuter and Dick Stillman and Ed LaChapelle.

The avalanche over, LaChapelle has been miraculously spared. Getting up, he walks slowly off slope.

CHAPTER 24

READY...
SET...GO

Snowshoe Thomson certainly was the most famous of the early California skiers; in fact, he is the only one people remember. Probably he was the first skier in the Sierra; he made his maiden run at Placerville in 1855. Of these honors, Snowshoe was proudly aware. But on February 21, 1869, he became aware, very sadly aware, of something else. He was not the best. While Snowshoe had been learning to dodge trees and jump over precipices in the course of his mail route, a

bunch of other Forty-niners had been holding straight downhill races for fun and cash (next pages). The best of them, according to California ski historian Robert H. Power, were the Sierra Boys of the Alturas Snowshoe Club (above), and they didn't mind who knew it. Theirs was a conceit that Snowshoe Thomson could not endure. He announced his participation in the Alturas Club's Third Annual Race, and for a warmup he skied a good part of the 200 miles from his home in Silver City to the race site in La Porte. That was as warm as Snowshoe ever got.

In the first event, he wound up in a heap outside the course markers, and in the next race he ran last. With that, the great man grumpily departed, trailing behind him a challenge to a rematch that would include a jump and a deep-woods slalom. And he threw in a heavy personal sidebet — to which the president of the Alturas Club replied that Thomson was a money-grubbing
continued

Hunched in antediluvian version of the modern Egg Position, four Sierra racers head for finish line.

sorehead. Furthermore, the Alturas Snowshoe boys were now certain they had nothing more to prove vis-à-vis Thomson, since "Doc Brewster has a mule that has been practising this winter on snowshoes that can beat him on an even string, and we have a Chinaman that can discount him."

232

The winners hoist a few at bottom of slope. Amateurism was unknown in these days and only training requirement was to show up.

A few of the boys gag it up for the photographer near the bottom of the downhill course at Table Rock tract in Howland Flat, Calif.

233

Wild Friars of Hanover

Between the running of the last race of the ancient series at La Porte, Calif., in 1911 and the beginning of World War II, there were very few ski races of any consequence in the U. S. that were not started and subsequently dominated by a group of dashing young men from the Dartmouth Outing Club. The outing club was founded in Hanover, N. H., in December 1909 by a Dartmouth junior named Fred Harris, who, like most other U. S. ski pioneers, found himself bored stiff in winter. The following season the club put on the first of its famous winter carnivals. Three years later, with the help of a couple of ringers from Hanover High School, the DOC split honors with McGill University in the first intercollegiate ski meet ever held; Dartmouth won the cross-country, McGill the jump. In 1923, again in a meet with McGill, Dartmouth Professor Charles Proctor laid out the first between-the-poles slalom ever run in the U. S. And, in 1927, the club sponsored

the first organized downhill since La Porte: the Moosilauke Downmountain, a hair-raising 2.8-mile affair which evolved, in 1933, into the first national downhill championship. By this time the outing club team also had evolved into the Dartmouth team, which, first under a delightful German named Otto Schniebs and later under the shrewd Walter Prager, exercised an iron rule over intercollegiate skiing. For that matter, from 1936 to 1940, the men on the Dartmouth teams – A. L. Washburn, Ted Hunter, Dave and Steve Bradley, Johnny Litchfield, Warren and Howard Chivers, Dick and Jack Durrance – were *the* power in U. S. racing, and made the first appreciable dent in the European circuit: Dick Durrance's eighth in the combined downhill and slalom at the 1936 Olympics in Garmisch remained the highest finish in Alpine racing by an American male until another Dartmouth man, Bill Beck, got a fifth place at Oslo in 1952.

Coach Otto Schniebs (left, above) leads charge by hell-bent racers of Dartmouth Outing Club. Though lacking refinements of style, outing club heroes were best native American skiers in the U. S. during the 1930's.

Greatest of the old Dartmouth skiers was Dick Durrance (below), who won three Harriman Cup races, the last in 1940 over the hair-raising Warm Springs course with an average speed of 48 mph.

ONE FOR THE ROAD

While men's racing in the U. S. acquired a certain early glamour through the exploits of the Hanover Hill Mob, women's competition remained an obscure form of amusement for a few close friends. Then on March 8, 1941, at Aspen, a tiny 22-year-old bride from Sun Valley named Gretchen Fraser, showing a style and drive that a male might envy, flashed through the slalom gates to win the national women's downhill championship. The next season she took the slalom. There was, now, only one thing left for this quick, graceful girl: to win a major international race, something no U. S. skier had ever managed. The war put a stop to all ski competition for four years, and it seemed that her chance was past. By the time of the first postwar Olympics at St. Moritz in 1948, Gretchen was 29, an age when most women racers are long gone back to the kitchen. Not Mrs. Fraser. After the second run of the slalom, she was the winner of a Winter Olympic gold medal, the first American to achieve that honor. *Then* she headed for the kitchen: "I'm definitely quitting skiing," she said—and did.

Any European who took comfort from Gretchen Fraser's retirement should have looked a little farther down the list of Olympic finishers. In 8th place in the slalom was a skinny 15-year-old from Rutland, Vt., Andrea Mead, who came down the mountain as though death were just behind her and someone she disliked very much just ahead. Four years later, at Oslo, though now only 19, she had become the best girl skier in the world, and was the favorite to win at least two events. She disappointed no one. She floated through the giant slalom as though she had invented the entire art of ski racing, to win by 2.2 seconds over her nearest competitor. In the slalom, she scrambled badly at one gate and was 1.2 seconds behind after the first heat. A teammate who stepped forward to encourage her took one look at the cold grey eyes and thought better of it.

"GET OUTTA MY WAY"

This would have been like encouraging a starving cheetah to strike down a passing goat. And in the second run, Andy came down just like a cheetah — cat-quick and deadly purposeful. Her time was, by .8 second, the best of the day, and her reward a second gold medal. It was the finest performance ever by a U. S. skier, and it really seemed that Andy Mead would be the sport's ruling queen for the next ten years. Instead, she went home to Vermont with her new husband, Dave Lawrence, and started having babies. This distressed many ski connoisseurs (five years later Austria's great Toni Sailer said sadly, "She is still the best if she vould just schtop having babies"), but it made the Lawrences happy. Mrs. Lawrence never did "schtop" having babies (there are now five), and America has never seen another skiing competitor the like of Andy Mead.

A BURDEN OF PROOF

At the mid-January training camp for Olympic prospects in Sun Valley in 1955, everyone was watching Jill Kinmont. She was worth it. Less than a year before, she had become, at 18, the only person ever to win the women's National Junior *and* Senior slalom in the same year. At Sun Valley, she looked like prime Olympic material, and George Macomber and Christian Pravda,

At Olympic camp in 1955, Jill Kinmont was most promising skier. She also seemed to have more fun than anyone else — skiing, flirting with men's star Buddy Werner (above), and laughing with girl friends.

238

special coaches at the camp, kept a close eye on her as she swung through practice on Baldy Mountain. Every other man was watching her because she was the prettiest girl in the place.

All this attention was a bit embarrassing to Jill, a snub-nosed blonde who seemed to think everyone was wonderful, and who skied simply because "it's so much fun." But Jill still had something to prove. When she won her Senior slalom title, the veteran U. S. racers — Katy Rodolph *et al.* — were in Sweden racing for the Federation Internationale du Ski world championship. On January 30, 1955, at Alta, Utah, she got her chance in the annual Snow Cup. The field included Andy Lawrence, Katy Rodolph, Skeeter Werner — all the good ones. The course, soft in the morning, had turned icy and very fast. A strong wind was blowing downhill as Andy Lawrence approached Jill at the top of the hill, smiled like a big sister, and said, "Take it easy."

Then Andy slid into the starting gate, and, with astonishing control over the dangerous run, set a time of 1:38.4, too good, really, for anyone to beat. Jill tried. Going off 15th, 11 positions behind Andy, she quickly—too quickly—climbed into high gear. Coming off the shoulder of Rustler Run, she bounced off a bump, shot 50 feet in the air, came down, somersaulted through some pine trees, grazed one spectator and knocked him 15 yards down the mountain. Finally, she stopped, and lay still in the snow, her eyes wide with fear. "Oh, my God," she said. "What have I done?" Then: "I can't feel anything."

Nor could she. Her fourth, fifth, and sixth cervical vertebrae were smashed, the spinal cord depressed, her body paralyzed. The ski patrol gently put her on a sled, and walked her down the hill. As the toboggan was being lifted into an ambulance, a grief-stricken Andy Lawrence said softly to Jill, "Gee, tiger, what were you doing?" Jill smiled and turned her eyes to the men carrying the toboggan. "Maybe you ought to carry me through the finish line, at least," she said.

That was almost nine years ago. Today, after an agony of therapy, Jill can use her arms, but she lives in a wheel chair. Nevertheless, she lives a vigorous, productive life, fairly bubbling with good humor. In 1962, she studied psychology at UCLA, and eight hours a week she taught remedial reading to children ten through 12. Now living in Seattle, she dates regularly, still makes pilgrimages with friends to Mammoth Mountain to

Six months later, body and legs paralyzed from accident, she smiled through therapy to gain use of arms.

visit with her first coach, Dave McCoy. "I couldn't be better," she told a reporter recently. On second thought, she admitted to some sadness over the low estate of the UCLA football team. Other than that, "I'm too busy to have any problems."

239

REQUIEM FOR A DAREDEVIL

During the 1950's, America's male racers failed to keep pace with the women. The men were held back partly by maladministration (right *et seq.*), and partly by terribly bad luck. Perhaps the most talented, and certainly the most exciting, skier during the first half of the decade was Dick Buek, a handsome, reckless young man who, by his own admission, thought of danger as a toy. "When I go out," he once told his fiancée, "I want to go big." And he meant it. By the winter of 1952, Buek had earned his first national downhill title and a reputation as a daredevil who would try anything — on skis, on a motorcycle, in a plane, or whatever. In May, 1953, he drove a motorcycle head-on into an onrushing automobile. Somehow he lived, but was told he would never ski again; and nine months later, reckless as ever, won his second downhill title. In March, 1955, he broke his back while training at Stowe, later reinjured it in a 40-foot fall during a summer job as a telephone lineman. Still, his upper body in a metal brace, he finished third in the 1956 downhill. Then, on Nov. 3, 1957, Dick Buek went out for keeps. It was a day of snow flurries; Buek and a friend decided this would be the day to practice stalls 200 feet over 6000-foot-high Donner Lake in a light airplane. The police pulled both men out of the floating remains of the wrecked plane. Both were dead before the rescuers had arrived, Buek of a broken neck.

REQUIEM FOR A SNAFU

Of all the skiing nations of the world, for the past 12 years only Austria has produced more natural talent than the U. S. But no nation has surpassed the U. S. in the fumble-fingered handling of its racers. The worst example among many was the selection of the 1956 Olympic squad, in which Bill Beck, top finisher among the U. S. males at Oslo (fifth in downhill) and the steadiest downhill racer in the nation, was left off the squad. On the day of the final race to determine who would make the team, the selection committee was still squabbling about how the team would be chosen. During the confusion, Beck (above) got the news that he hadn't made it. His erstwhile teammates were so enraged that Beck eventually was put on the squad where he belonged. But it was a demoralized squad and it did badly in the Winter Games at Cortina, Italy.

DENVER'S DRILLMASTER

The menacing figure above, glowering in a perfectionist's displeasure at the nation's finest college ski team, is Willy Schaeffler, who is probably more things to more people than anyone else in the ski world. To the Europeans who came to the Squaw Valley Olympics, he is a genius for the quality of the racing courses he, as Director of Ski Events, prepared under impossible conditions. To the men working under him at Squaw, he was "der Führer," a martinet who never seemed to know when too much work was enough. To the racers on his University of Denver ski teams, which long ago captured dominance of intercollegiate skiing from Dartmouth,

he is a driving tutor and a merciless conditioner. One former Denver captain admitted he "sometimes wanted to challenge Willy." Instead, the racers went out and won for him, thinking at the time that they won in anger, realizing later they won out of loyalty and affection. To the mass of American skiers he is the prophet of the short-swing, the man who did the most to modernize ski technique in the U. S. To his friends, even his closest friends, he is a mystery, vanishing for weeks at a time, popping up in Europe, New York, the Rockies, California, sometimes warm, sometimes tough, but always somehow remote. More than anything, he is Willy Schaeffler, of whom there is but one, and without whom the sport of skiing in America would be much the less.

THE BEST EVER?

In late 1953, a scared kid named Wallace (Buddy) Werner from Steamboat Springs, Colo., won a race in the tryouts for the 1954 FIS team. But when the traveling squad was picked, Werner, then only 17, was left home; too young, the coaches said. Then a regular broke his leg during the European swing, and officials frantically cabled Werner to join the team. He did, and promptly beat Europe's best in a race in Norway. For the next six years, at any moment of any given day, Buddy Werner was the fastest skier in the world. The only trouble was that the moment was usually during the first half of a race, just before the rocketing Werner took one of the hair-raising spills for which he became famous. When-

ever he managed to stand up all the way, he won: the Grand Prix de Chamonix Downhill in 1956, the Lauberhorn Combined in 1958, the Hahnen-kamm Downhill in 1959. But there were too many pratfalls between the prizes for Buddy to get the top world rating of which he was capable. Late in the winter of 1959, he steadied down, skiing flawlessly to win the downhill and slalom and finishing second in the giant slalom at the North American championships. Buddy had matured. The Olympics were approaching, and he was ready. So was fate. Two months before the Games, he broke his leg, losing his best—and perhaps last—chance for a medal. "He was the only foreigner we were worried about," said Austria's coach Othmar Schneider. "It will be a long time before America has another skier as good."

Les Girls

"I'm 36–25–38," said Penny Pitou to *Sports Illustrated* writer Roy Terrell in January of 1960, "and if you don't think I'm in condition, just feel that." She banged a fist against a solid thigh. "She's a tiger," said Bill Beck, coach of the U. S. men's team. "She's also quite a girl."

Penny, a bouncy blonde from Gilford, N. H., was not the only determined, talented, and pretty girl who had risen to the top of U. S. skiing that year. In fact she was only one of a crowd that in-

Friend of Betsy Snite through part of her whirlwind winter of 1959 was Austrian ace Josl Rieder.

Light of Penny Pitou's life during same winter, and now till death do them part, is Egon Zimmermann.

cluded Betsy Snite, Sally Deaver, Linda Meyers, Beverly Anderson, and Joan Hannah. Every girl in the crowd had two things in common: good looks and an ability to beat the world's best. Three of them shared another attribute: the ability to collect Austrian boy friends who provided them not only companionship, but also the best free ski coaching available anywhere.

"Maybe that sounds funny," said Snite to Terrell, "but it's important. It's not so much that they *teach* you how to ski properly, *they* show you. You're standing there on the top of the mountain, looking down this absolutely dizzy run, and sud-

denly they say, 'Let's go,' and they're gone. You learn to ski fast, or you spend a lonesome winter." During the winter of 1959, which they spent in Europe, Betsy and Penny certainly learned to ski fast, picking up racing medals at Grindelwald, Kitzbühel, and Garmisch, among other places. Deaver, the national women's slalom champion in 1956 and 1957, raced in Europe in 1958, but stayed in the U. S. through 1959. When she showed up at Squaw Valley for the North Americans, she got Austrian racer Toni Marth to act as her coach.

Marth, however, turned out to be a less successful coach than Penny's private Austrian, Egon Zimmermann, or Betsy's Josl Rieder. Sally failed the next January to make the Olympic team. But Betsy and Penny were very much on the team, backed by Meyers, Hannah, Anderson, and a newcomer named Renie Cox. It was, potentially, the strongest women's team ever fielded. Both Snite and Pitou were rated as good bets for gold medals; and it was not impossible to think the U. S. team would sweep all three events.

Though their teammates won no medals at the Olympics, Penny and Betsy very nearly made their sweep. In the downhill, watched by a greater audience than had ever before seen a ski event — 240,904 in the valley and 96,000,000 on national TV — Penny tore down the course, faltered for an instant at one turn, and finished second by that instant. In the giant slalom, she took another close second. For her part, Betsy finished second in the slalom. Then both girls promptly retired from racing to do what they wanted to do most, Penny to marry Egon, and Betsy to return to the social whirl ("I was put on this earth to be a female") of her long-neglected secretary-model job in the very social city of San Francisco.

Sally Deaver, killed in tragic horseback accident this fall, skied at Squaw Valley with Austrian Toni Marth

245

Millennium for U. S. Ski Racing

Ever since the U. S. stumbled into international competition with Sigurd Overby's 12th-place finish in the 18-km. cross country at the first Winter Olympics at Chamonix in 1924, the life of an American ski coach has been one of poverty and despair. For example, listen to Friedl Pfeifer, who coached what passed for the U. S. ladies' team at the 1956 Olympics: "I mean I was the coach of the ladies' team at Cortina, and was not appointed until three months before the race. And the whole thing hits you in the face. The coach should get $5000, plus expenses. Now, he gets nothing. They send you a letter 'Greetings,' like Uncle Sam. You can turn it down, but it makes you a slob. It cost me $3000 out of my own pocket to go to Cortina, and this is an intolerable situation."

No less so for Bill Beck, whose career as an Olympic competitor was bitter enough (see page 241), but nothing to the slings and arrows he endured after being appointed coach of the U. S. men's team for 1960. An Easterner, Beck found the U. S. Olympic committee hedging on his request for $500 so he could travel west to see the boys who would be racing for him.

Nor did Dave Lawrence find the going any smoother, either as the ladies' coach in 1960, or as a team member in previous years. "Did Friedl say $3000?" Lawrence asked. "It cost me that in Squaw Valley. They approached me again this winter and I said, 'Baloney.' Andy and I feel that racing has always been a bastard stepchild of the NSA or USSA or whatever it is now. They've always nickeled and dimed racing to death. Because it's on a volunteer basis, and subject to Association politics, with no continuity. The coach has the team picked for him, and he doesn't have the authority. In Europe, in 1958, for the FIS when Pepi Gabl was the coach, Noni Foley skied poorly in the early races. She was unhappy. She should have been sent home. But Pepi couldn't do it because of fear of reaction. In 1952, when Suzy Harris Rytting, who had

Coach Bob Beattie shares a victory smile with Joan Hannah, who performed well on European swing.

been married some time before the trip, was pregnant and was sent home, the papers let out a tremendous blast.

"The coach should have absolute authority over the team. And the appointment should be for three to five years. Not just one year."

These words were spoken in February, 1962, and they were spoken with a rare combination of passion and justification. Recreational skiing in the U. S. had grown in public interest, general skill and dollar investment far beyond the level of skiing in any other country in the world. Sports — national teams — had become an important part of international diplomacy. Yet the U. S. teams, because they were organized by short-term volunteers, financed by last-minute tin-cup shaking, and further afflicted by a severe ideological hangover from the dear, dead days when an amateur was a self-supporting gentleman who must never, never compete against the village cow-

246

herd, were really no better than they were in 1950. Anyone who tried to make them better by striking at the heart of the problem got precious little thanks from the body of the U. S. Ski Association. In 1960 Sepp Ruschp, then president of the association, tried to reform the entire fiscal program of the organization by creating strong vertical financing from the clubs up through the national (as is done in Europe), by starting a separate and perpetual fund to use for international competition only (as is done in Europe), and by ringing in ski equipment manufacturers for fat contributions (as is certainly done in Europe). For his pains he was harassed into resigning, having succeeded only in establishing the fund which was, of course, woefully undersubscribed. Thus Friedl Pfeifer, Sepp Ruschp, Bill Beck, Dave Lawrence *et al.,* were inclined toward despair early in 1962, since there seemed to be no prospect that anything good would ever happen to improve the structure of U. S. ski racing.

Oddly, at that moment, something very good was already happening. An American team was in Europe, six men and five women, training for the FIS World Championships in France that February. At first glance, this U. S. team seemed like any other. It had left home with only part of the funds it needed for the round trip, and no assurance that the balance would be forthcoming. A few talented veterans, among them Buddy Werner and Linda Myers, did well in the early meets, but the team as a whole looked none too powerful; coach Bob Beattie, of the University of Colorado, had never traveled abroad with a team, let alone led one through the intricacies of European ski diplomacy.

Yet this team turned out to be like nothing the U. S. had ever had before, and it presaged a complete change in American racing. Under the adroit and persuasive handling of a new financial chairman, Ralph Des Roches, the paltry $11,000 in the competition fund grew to a hefty $85,000 — oversubscribed by $30,000. Beattie turned out to be anything but a half-lost, kid-glove handler of prima donnas. He treated the skiers for what they were: youngsters who wanted to win and needed close handling to do it. And if he loaded his skiers with some painful clichés ("When the going gets tough, the tough get tougher"), he also loaded them with a spirit and confidence rare indeed among American ski teams. Result: seven victories in major meets.

More important, however, was the outlook for the future. Beattie was not just coach of that season's FIS team. He was going to be the U. S. Olympic team coach for 1964; and here he was, two years ahead of time, working with his skiers. Better still, back home a group of Chicago-area businessmen, at the suggestion of Willy Schaeffler, were raising a tax-free fund called the Skiers Training Trust, independent of USSA politicking, to be used exclusively for the training of racers. In December of 1962, a $10,000 allotment from the fund financed the first off-season training camp for Olympic candidates. For two weeks at Vail, Colo., which donated its lift facilities for the effort, some six dozen of America's best young racers worked out under their own coaches at the Trust's expense. Beattie, who along with the other coaches was getting a well-earned $100 a week plus expenses, supervised the over-all effort. During the remainder of the winter, 13 Olympic tryout races were held on a clearly defined basis for qualification. The climax was at the 1963 National championships, held at a brand-new area called Alyeska, just outside Anchorage, Alaska. There, at a meet extraordinarily well organized and well run for the United States, let alone for Alaska which had never before held a national championship of any kind, Buddy Werner won the downhill and giant slalom to prove he was still the best all-around skier in America. The slalom winner was Chuck Ferries, who the previous winter had become the first U. S. racer ever to win the slalom at a top European meet. Naturally, they made the team. Behind them were 12 other well-qualified youngsters. Moreover, Beattie had a strong hand in the choosing of the skiers; and, wonder of wonders, he also picked his own assistants. The U. S. coach was, finally, the boss of the U. S. team.

As for the money, with Des Roches still in charge, it kept rolling in — from the Training Trust, from ski areas like Sun Valley and Sepp Ruschp's Mt. Mansfield Co., Inc., and from a lot of strange and previously unwelcome sources like Ski Industries America, an association of equipment manufacturers.

It seems finally to have occurred to American ski officials that all who make money from skiing are not evil, and that an equipment manufacturer or an area operator can give more to racing than a bad name. Mainly, it seems finally to have occurred that, in racing at least, the Organization should be, above all things, Organized.

CHAPTER 25

ONE FOR THE MONEY

A vision of horror to amateur officials, pro racing boss Friedl Pfeifer happily shows off winner's loot.

On Jan. 29, 1961, Friedl Preifer took a bundle of green bills from his pocket and waved them happily in the air. Then, with the broadest of smiles, he handed the money — all $1500 of it — to ski instructor Christian Pravda, who had just beaten 11 other racers in a downhill on Buttermilk Mountain. With this act of largesse, Pfeifer launched professional ski racing in the U. S., and with it the worst hassle in the hassle-ridden history of U. S. ski racing.

"Now no racer needs to be a hypocrite any more," said Toni Spiss, who picked up $400 for finishing third. "He doesn't have to race for money under the table or for some ski manufacturer," Spiss continued. "He can race right out in the open for dollars, and I'm glad."

"I am very much in favor of this," said Sigi Engl, the shrewd and voluble head of the Sun Valley Ski School. "It will give the boys who gave so much for their country in racing, those boys who worked so hard, those boys will have a chance to make some money before they become a trainer or what. I think it's a good thing for skiing."

"We skiers now admit openly that we're earning money," said Stein Eriksen, once an Olympic and FIS medal winner for Norway, and at present a part-time member of the professional racing troupe.

From the amateurs, there came a counterblast whose echoes are still rolling off the peaks of the leading ski areas from Vermont to the Pacific Coast. "It is . . . a threat to amateur sport," wrote Roland Palmedo, the implacable enemy of any racer rash enough to pick up his money at the finish line. Another purist, J. Stanley Mullin, wrote darkly of the thrown fight in professional boxing, leaving little doubt in the reader's mind that this also would happen in professional skiing. The cannonade could have been predicted from Palmedo and Mullin, two men with long-standing concern (see pages 252–253), official and otherwise, for the health and welfare of amateur racing. But there was one bit of counterfire that was totally unexpected. It came from Hans Peter Lanig, who apparently estimated his own amateurism to be as pure as the silver medal he won in the downhill at Squaw Valley. "The dollar rules America," wrote Lanig, who was not long gone from a job at the ski-conscious Broadmoor Hotel, where he had been hired following the Olympics. "This materialistic mentality had to have its bad effect on American skiing. The

After a long, sad year of warring with the amateurs, Pfeifer jumps for joy as one of his Aspen racers, Anderl Molterer, wins first world pro championship.

future of amateur skiing may be imperiled. . . . Instead of the Olympics there will be pro racing only, with skiers wearing the names of their sponsoring manufacturers on their chests."

"*Ja,*" rumbled Willy Schaeffler, perhaps the most fearless spade-caller in skiing. "It's too bad we can't all be millionaires. *Ja,* the purists. The so-called pro hunters."

When Friedl started the business of pro racing, he had no intention of stirring up such a wasp's nest. In fact, his charter for the International Professional Ski Racers Association, governing body for the pros, specifically stated that no amateur racer under the age of 24 could enter an IPSRA race. Since most crack amateurs have quit racing by 24, Pfeifer hoped this provision would put various minds at rest about any possible raiding by the pros. To further ease the situation, he inserted another clause forbidding a skier to enter an IPSRA event in the same season he raced as an amateur.

The main purpose for pro racing was to make money. From a ski racer's point of view, it was not an ignoble purpose. Before Friedl handed the money to Christian Pravda, only two ski racers had ever been able to get a quick return when they quit being amateurs. Stein Eriksen signed himself into a succession of profitable deals, and now makes over $30,000 selling ski clothes and equipment and running the ski school at Aspen Highlands. Toni Sailer, the only triple gold-medal winner in Olympic ski history, picked up $125,000 from a book, records, films, a hotel, and a textile business in the first three years after he quit. The others have, for the most part, drifted into $20-a-day jobs teaching skiing, or have gone back to the farm. Now, with the professional racing, the odds are a little better, and the money is beginning to spread out more evenly. In the opening season, there were only six races. But in the second year there were 10 events with

continued

total prize money of $45,000, the big winner being Aspen instructor Anderl Molterer, who picked up $12,425 in purses and endorsements. Ernst Hinterseer, Pravda, and Pepi Gramshammer were not far behind.

With this kind of quick growth, plus endorsements from Head Ski and White Stag clothing, and a peak crowd of 11,500 willing to spend $1.50 apiece to stand around in the snow and watch a two-day meet at Heavenly Valley, IPSRA should have been set for a prosperous life. But it was not. Instead, Pfeifer found himself fighting a long and sometimes desperate siege.

At its annual meeting in May, 1962, the USSA resolved that any club or person who helped organize or put on a pro race was through in amateur skiing. Furthermore, any club official who was involved in a pro race, no matter where, automatically disqualified his entire club. And there was another, prior, move afoot to disqualify any ski area which put on a pro race.

This was a bitter blow, and it caught the pros by surprise, and below the belt. "A week after the first pro race," said Friedl, "I was down to the Broadmoor to set a slalom there. And there was Marc Hodler (then head of the FIS), Sepp Ruschp (then still president of the USSA), and Stanley Mullin. So it was a good chance for me to find out what they think. Sepp didn't say much. But Marc Hodler says, 'I am not opposed. I see things, I have reservations, but I am not opposed.' And he gave me a copy of the FIS rule book, autographed. Stan Mullin said, 'I am for it. It makes a division — one is white, the other is black — if you want to say it that way. I am in favor of this.' But then they went back, and now I am having trouble with one of them."

Stein Eriksen was even more bitter about the attack on the pros. "Now, I will tell you what I think about that and what is the truth. When I was down there at the Broadmoor, I was in the car with this amateur official and he could *hardly contain* his enthusiasm for pro racing. But now I think he feels he cannot be in favor of pro racing. And what I think is this distinguished gentleman sitting next to me in the car is a phony. Now I don't want to be sued for that, but I have these two people who were there and will back me up as to what he said."

Later, Friedl said, "We have always, *always,* said we wanted to help support amateur skiing. We are giving the Aspen Ski Club more than $1000, and we give something to the FIS competion fund. What sport, can you tell me, what sport is there today without an elite group of pros at the top? Golf? They got *millions* of golfers. And who is carrying that? A small group of pros at the top that everybody looks up to.

"Look, in skiing I have been a pro for twenty years, but in setting courses and acting as a race official I have been amateur. Look at Squaw Valley. All we who set those courses and did things, we were all pros. So what do they mean?"

Sepp Ruschp had a pretty good idea just what they meant. "One of these men is the head of defending amateurism and yet he owned a large interest in a chair lift, which he sold at an enormous profit. And he endorses books. Why are we penalizing the son of the poor man who needs the money to be a racer? Who gets all the benefit is the son of the rich man. He is an amateur because his father can afford it."

And back to Friedl: "These amateurs, oh, yes, they all get paid anyway. One of the racers here in Aspen told me they used to give him money — paid him. All the racers are supposed to get is skis. But this racer told me they gave him cash. Another one was Toni Sailer. I myself gave Toni Sailer $3000 to ski here in 1957. That was before the FIS, and he was already negotiating contracts, but he was supposed to be an amateur."

Sailer's subsequent fencing with amateur officials provided one of the great chapters in the saga of purism. He avoided the letter of the law in one movie by appearing on water skis instead of snow skis. And in another picture his acting was said, somewhat facetiously, to be so amateurish that he could not possibly be called a professional.

This sort of thing is neither ancient history nor is it confined to Austrian racers. As recently as 1962 a French racer, sounded out on the possibility of his turning pro, said, "Why should I when I can make so much more as an amateur?" In the same year France's all-time great ski ace Guy Perillat appeared smilingly on the jacket of a 45-rpm recording (which was not given away), on which he sang *L'Amour Me Brule* and *Tais-Toi* about as well as Toni Sailer acts. Lest acceptance of money be thought endemic only to foreigners and/or those who subsequently teamed up with Pfeifer, it is worth pointing out that as long ago as 1951, Janette Burr, George Macomber, and Dave and Andy Lawrence, as U. S. amateurs racing in Austria, were given not only over-ocean-and-back expenses, border-to-border expenses while in Austria, but also $40 a week for general fun and games. All the Austrian, and presumably all the American, amateur officials knew it; but no one said a word, possibly because this passage of money—unlike Pfeifer's money—posed no threat to the established Organization's control of top-level racing. As for the matter of free ski equipment, which has always been allowed under the amateur code, a member of the U. S. team received some 15 pairs of skis during his trip to Cortina in 1956. He shipped all 15 pairs home, and, according to common practice, sold practically all of them at 100 per cent profit. The Koestle ski firm now gives only three pairs of wooden skis to any member of any national team which requests them; but the promotional emphasis on these skis is still unamateurishly strong: Marianne Jahn's first words, on winning at Chaminox, were, "I could not have done it without my wooden skis" (the pros were pushing metal skis at the time).

Looking back at the tangled past, and ahead to the stormy future, Dave Lawrence summed up the attitude of most informed skiers on the pro hassle: "Amateurism in ski racing is a thing of the past. And these guys — Palmedo and company — are going through life with blinders on if they can't see it. Until we get an open relationship — not open racing right away, although that would be terrific — between the pros and amateurs, we'll never get anywhere. Look at what has been happening lately in tennis. Those amateur characters have *killed* tennis. And, if we're not careful, they're going to do the same thing to skiing."

CHAPTER 26

THE OTHER

ROLAND PALMEDO

Roland Palmedo, shown right at Squaw Valley talking to Friedl Pfeifer, his arch-opponent in ski-racing philosophy, is by profession a very successful investment banker. His real passion, however, is skiing, both as a participant sport and as a means to physical fitness. As he clearly indicates here, he is dead set against anything — professional skiing, steam heat, school buses, or power-driven lawn mowers — that may contribute to the softening of the national fiber:

"How are we to avoid becoming a nation of flabby, weak, physically timid, pear-shaped softies? (In 1960, draft rejection rate for physical, mental and moral reasons was *73 per cent.*)

"What more practical and pleasant way than by sports, particularly competitive sports and outdoor life, plus the regard for condition, training and health that sports encourage?

"If this is so, then we see that the true function and objective of sport should not be primarily to develop world champions or to furnish thrilling entertainment. The chance to become a world champion — or a national champion, or a local champion, for that matter — should be an incentive and reward to the best of a whole broad-based pyramid of competitors. The whole sports structure should be an encouragement to take part. Providing entertainment by professional competitors, such as do baseball or basketball, is a business, not a sport. As a legitimate business it must try to make fans rather than participants, create customers rather than players.

"Any leisure occupation or entertainment that discourages participation is an adverse influence, except to the extent that it offers other benefits, educational or cultural, for instance.

"This does not imply that professional baseball is any less a legitimate business than a candy store, or that a professional hockey player is any less to be respected as a wage earner than a band leader or a trapeze artist.

"But what benefit is derived by 2000 or 4000

J. STANLEY MULLIN

Stanley Mullin, a Los Angeles lawyer, is a director of the USSA, vice president of the FIS, and, most important, chairman of the FIS Eligibility Committee. He is shown, right, talking with professional racer Christian Pravda. Here is what he thinks about the pros:

"All amateur sport is extremely broad based, going to the lowest levels of competitive ability and to the lowest level of ages — the objective has always been, the more that participate the better.

"Competing for money prizes is, on the other hand, oriented toward a completely different objective. Here, the objective is to provide a cash reward for the winner. To provide the cash reward, a gate must be provided which will yield sums necessary for the rewards. As a consequence, the event must have theatrical characteristics or the public will not attend. The paying public is not interested in watching Juniors, Sub-Juniors, Classes D, C, and B — it is interested only in the topflight competitors and, therefore, the field is limited to a few. In professional ski racing, IPSRA has admitted this fact very openly by announcing that only ten Class A members will be accepted at any one time.

"Because the end objective is money, the pressure for cutting corners is injected in the professional sports in a manner far beyond that of amateur sports competitions. Having participated in a mild way in sports car racing, I personally know the difference between the attitude of a driver competing for money and a driver competing for the honor, esteem and prestige of being a winner.

"Professional ski racing is not to be compared to professional tennis or professional golf — in the latter two events, a very different set of facts exists. In professional tennis, we have a highly developed theatrical situation with an audience, and today professional golf tournaments have risen to be very large audience attractions. In both cases, you have a considerable number of

SIDE SPEAKS OUT

young Americans watching six or eight foreign pro stars race? Isn't it rather stultifying for American universities to recruit their ski teams in Scandinavia?

"I don't know who coined the word 'spectatoritis,' but it was J. Edgar Hoover who referred to this pastime as one of the evidences of the 'deterioration disease' that is undermining American physical fitness.

"I think it should be realistically recognized that the amateur competitor in world events must be given a fair and reasonable opportunity to train into top physical condition and also to develop his skill to the peak of his ability, within reasonable limits of time. At the same time, excesses, such as the encouragement of 'career competitors' may perhaps best be avoided by limiting training and practice periods.

"Let us . . . encourage sports for the greatest good for the greatest number of Americans, and not let this objective be frustrated by ulterior, mercenary, selfish, or shortsighted policies."

spectators who thereby hope to learn something which they themselves can use in sport — and practically all of these *competing* professionals are at the same time *teaching* or *coaching* professionals. This is not true in professional ski racing where the physical risks involved are not at all the same as in golf and tennis and where the danger of injury is so great that a professional career can be brought precipitously to a close and the participant left high and dry.

"Some writers today, in referring to the present professional ski racing circus, refer to the fact that participants were 'saved' from the life of a ski instructor. I think this is somewhat libelous in view of the fact that there are many excellent ski teachers who have achieved a status comparable to successful businessmen. I am sure you are personally acquainted with Sepp Ruschp of Stowe, Sigi Engl of Sun Valley, and Friedl Pfeifer of Aspen — and I would not say that these men had been harmed in their business careers by the fact that they were 'ski teachers' in the beginning."

PART IV

Photographs by Toni Frissell

THE FUN OF SKIING

In all the heavy breathing about athletes, eligibility, and money, people sometimes forget that the only real reason for skiing is to have fun. If some young skiers like to race, fine. And if others enjoy teaching them, or organizing the competitions, so much the better. But the racers and organizers, though they have done so much to publicize the sport, are no more than a platoon in a vast army of winter vacationers, most of whom don't care whether anyone ever wins another race. In fact, some of the racers feel that way themselves. For example, Skeeter Werner (right), whom some coaches once considered as talented a racer as her redoubtable brother Buddy, long ago decided it was more fun to be a pretty girl on an Aspen sundeck than a fire-breathing downhill specialist. Brooks Dodge (page 259), who got a fourth in the slalom at the 1956 Olympics, seems just as happy playing king of Tuckerman's Ravine. As the following pages show, there are numberless other ways in which America's 2,000,000 recreational skiers have fun without ever putting a foot in a starting gate.

254

Tom Watson, Jr., board chairman of IBM, owns chalet at Stowe, finds family skiing — and a scramble in the snow — best way to relax from business.

Bruce Cardy hangs on to towline of pony as he spears ring in Richard Meek photograph taken at winter carnival in Steamboat Springs, Colo.

Photographs by Hanson Carroll

In early May skiers crowd onto the immense headwall at Tuckerman's Ravine. This is no sport for the old of limb or the faint of heart: the upper slopes of the wall are pitched at 55 degrees; there is no lift, no enclosed shelter beyond one cabin (left), and the nearest road is 2 miles from the cabin. However, for a strong, skillfull skier like Brooks Dodge (right), there is a special excitement to jump-turning down the headwall; and at night, around the campfires, there is a special pleasure for everyone else in just being there.

CHAPTER 27

PLACE IN THE SNOW

The brightly colored object nestled in the snow-bank at left has been called a number of things by a number of people. Creative architects, sneering at its uncomplicated lines, at the heat loss through the tremendous roof area, and just perhaps at the low price tag, have called it a split-level tepee. At least, that is the tag applied to it by Peter Blake, a skiing architect whose observations on the fine art of snow-country living begin below. To the contractors who put up the building, it is known as an A-frame, a good money-maker in the vacation house market. To its owners, it is the most popular version of what is fast becoming the proudest possession of many American families: a small, inexpensive private ski chalet.

Not all chalets are A-frame. In the town of Aspen alone, 135 individually designed ski houses have been put up in the past five years. Still, to those who dream of a second house, and who cannot afford a complicated individual design, the A-frame very probably is the most attractive standard model available. In fact, it has become so standard that prefabricators have begun to make the shells of A-frames, for shipment in packaged, panelized form, to just about any ski resort.

This picture shows one of the prefabbed A-frames sold by a Boston concern called Stanmar, Inc. The chalet has a 26-by-28-foot foundation, and costs only $3900 assembled on the buyer's lot. The total cost with the land and utilities was $10,000. When this A-frame went up in 1960, Stanmar already was doing an $800,000-a-year gross in vacation homes. By 1962, the figure had jumped to $2,000,000, and the following year the company budgeted for a 30 per cent increase over that. Stanmar has about 12 different kinds

Photograph by Ezra Stoller

Gordon Hall's A-frame at Mad River in Vermont has bedrooms and furnace in foundation, living room on first floor, dining room in balcony at rear.

of houses, both A-frame and post-and-beam construction, and, if the demand ever gets heavy enough, it is geared to put up as many as five houses in a single day. Recently, Stanmar got orders for three A-frames in Kingfield, Maine, hard by the Sugarloaf ski area; at the same time it was involved in negotiations for a 100-acre summer-house development in Martha's Vineyard in Massachusetts.

Other builders in Colorado, California, and the Northwest have gone into the A-frame business as well. For example, in the winter of 1959–60 a cluster of A-frames went up in Aspen at the foot of the Little Nell lift. Two years later, Frank Brown, scion of the Brown Tie and Lumber Company of McCall, Idaho, began selling prefab A-frames in Aspen for $11,000 and up *sans* land; and over the summer of 1962, contractor Wayne Handwerk put up a custom-built $23,000 A-frame near the middle of town. At Alpine Meadows in California, the A-frame is one of the reasons for the prosperity of Alpine Meadows Estates and the Bear Creek Association, two companies that already have sold or leased more than 500,000 dollars' worth of building lots near the ski lifts. No matter what the size or the price, however, the A-frame has arrived. So, too, have the other designs — miniature Swiss chalets, log cabins, Bavarian huts, and extravagant, glass-walled moderns.

The earlier ski chalets, the precursors of today's popular second houses, were custom jobs, $40,000-and-up. The Harriman Cottage at Sun Valley, the first real chalet in the country, could not be duplicated today for $40,000. In 1958 at Mad River, Godfrey Rockefeller put up a $50,000 beauty, complete with its own private chair lift to convey the family from the parking lot to the chalet. There are still a fair number of these gold-platers being built: Alexander McIlvaine designed a magnificent retreat at Sugarbush for Rocky Sack; and Larry Haess of Stowe did a modest-looking but very comfortable second

continued

house near Mt. Mansfield for IBM chairman Tom Watson. The big market today, however, is in volume production of prefabs and the smaller custom homes, in the $20,000 range. In the winter of 1962–63, by a wild guess, 350 of these smaller places appeared across the U. S., representing an investment of about $9,000,000.

One reason for this flourishing trade is that families are beginning to find the second house increasingly attainable. "Most of us skied at college," said one builder near Stowe, "and some of us were in the Tenth Mountain Division during the war. Before we married, we used to spend the week ends in ski lodges. Now we're older, have a few kids, and building our own chalets seems to be the logical thing to do."

Nancy Barnum, of New York, feels the same about a chalet that she and her husband built to share with another couple. "We used to rent an old farmhouse," she said, "but now we have children, and when you have a small child you want comfort. If there's a blizzard, you want to know everything will work, and that you aren't going to be sitting in the dark, freezing."

It seems that way to a lot of other skiers. They have discovered that it is quite possible to build a chalet for no more than $15,000 (including land) in or near most of the popular resorts — and get a bank to lend up to two-thirds of the necessary cash. This means $5000 down, or $2500 per family if two families go into the chalet. The mortgage cost per family is then only $36 per month on a 20-year mortgage. Considering that it often costs $15 to $20 per person per day (without meals) to stay at a hotel, the investment seems to make pretty good sense.

That, at least, is a growing belief: in Squaw Valley 125 houses have been built over the last five years; in the Ketchum area, near Sun Valley, 100 new houses went up during that same period.

Along with the demand for housing, land values in mountain areas have shot up. Land costs may range up to $140,000 per acre in the center of Aspen, where a minimum lot of 60 feet by 100 feet is all one can find. Such prices obviously will shatter any low chalet budget; the rule of thumb is that land should cost no more than 20 per cent of the budget. However, there are still some excellent properties within a radius of five miles of a ski lift, selling for less than the figure above. Friedl Pfeifer's Sleepy Hollow subdivision, near Buttermilk, opened recently with one- to two-acre

lots costing $4000 to $8000 cash. Near most of the New England resorts, improved land on a good road with electric and telephone lines can be bought for $1000 per acre. Unimproved land on back-country roads can be had for a little as $10 an acre.

Once the land has been acquired the new property owner faces two immediate expenses. The first is drilling a well (allow $1000); the other is digging a septic tank ($400). This need for private sewage disposal and a private water supply exists in almost all U. S. ski areas, since no more than two or three winter resorts have water lines or sewers along their village roads. One of the happy exceptions is the new area at Stratton Mountain, Vt., where the ski corporation allows lot buyers to hook into the community system for $2000 — not much more money, initially, than a well and septic tank but infinitely less trouble.

Suppose, then, that land, water, and septic tank total about $3000. The remaining $12,000 in a $15,000 budget should build a chalet of about 800 to 1000 square feet. A hefty chunk of the budget must go for insulation; a badly insulated house may cost up to $100 per month for heat or more than four times the bill for a good job. A good job includes double glazing — at least in windows facing north.

Every chalet should have a good fireplace. The cost may be anywhere from $500 for a concrete block job in New England to $3500 for a handsome stone fireplace in Sun Valley. Still, there is nothing like lounging about a real fireplace after a long day of skiing. Also, the fireplace will save on the heating bill.

Beyond these expenses the basic heating system (which should be either forced warm air or electric, neither of which will freeze up) will range from $250 to $1000. The interior plumbing system will cost about $800. Once these costs have been met, there will not be too much money left for the construction of the house itself, and anyone with a limited budget will have to economize somewhere. A good place to do this is in the sleeping area. Skiers don't seem to mind sleeping on double- or triple-decker bunks, cots, benches or floors.

However, most chalet designers feel that the best way to economize is in the over-all shape of the chalet. Dan Kiley, an architect who lives in Charlotte, Vt., is convinced, despite the popularity of the A-frame, that the way to build a good ski chalet is to make it square. This keeps the hard-to-heat exterior wall area to a minimum and allows the hot air inside the house to travel upward through every room, rather than collecting just under the apex of the peaked roof. Another advantage of the square house is that snow will blow off a flat roof before it has time to collect. On a peaked roof, wind eddies pile the snow on one side, where it will melt and freeze to the shingles, ultimately causing leaks. The Swiss and the Austrians, who have been living with snow and ice for a considerable time, also admire the flat or low-pitched roof. So, for that matter, does architect Blake.

There are only two further points to consider: maintenance and rentability. If the chalet is going to be occupied all winter, there should be little trouble with maintenance. Pipes are not likely to freeze as long as the heating system does not go on the blink. But if the chalet is to be used primarily on week ends, as most of them are, it is a good idea to find some reliable local person to act as caretaker, or else take all kinds of elaborate and expensive precautions, such as installing a stand-by generator and wrapping water pipes in heating tape.

The best thing for an absentee owner to do is to keep his place occupied by tenants. Depending upon how many skiers a chalet will sleep, it may bring from $750 and up per season, $200 and up per month, or upwards of $60 per week end. Few new owners will be as lucky in their rental rates as those in Squaw Valley, some of whom got back as much as 40 per cent of their building costs by renting during the 1960 Winter Games.

Even without a windfall like the Olympics, by giving up a month here and there, by renting over the big week ends when the lifts are too crowded for decent skiing, anyway, and perhaps by skipping one full season, the chalet owner can easily meet his tax and maintenance costs. He may also be able to take a big bite out of his mortgage, especially if he has built in an area which doubles as a summer resort.

With these added possibilities, of course, many new owners will discover that they have put up a house that is too profitable to live in themselves. They may then carry the second-house syndrome one step further and decide to build two chalets: the first to rent out, the other to live in. However they do it, they might try warming up their new place with one or two of the concoctions at right.

RECIPES

HOT BUTTERED RUM
According to Jean Mayer, Taos, N. Mex.

1 teaspoon brown sugar
1 teaspoon honey
⅛ teaspoon cinnamon
2 oz. light rum
4 oz. water
2 teaspoons butter

Mix brown sugar, honey, and cinnamon into a paste. Set paste in serving glass. Add two shots of good light rum, slightly heated. Put spoon in glass to keep from cracking, then fill with hot water. Add butter. If you want to finish with a flourish, super-heat the finished drink with a poker pulled from an open fireplace.

GLÜHWEIN
As served in the Ram, Sun Valley, Idaho

1 quart Burgundy or claret
4 strips lemon rind
3–4 strips orange rind
6 cloves
1 cinnamon stick
3–4 teaspoons cane sugar

In a copper, steel, or Pyrex pot, simmer the wine gently, so the alcohol doesn't boil off. Break the cinnamon stick and tie it, along with the rinds and other spices, in cheesecloth. Dunk condiments in simmering wine. When someone says it smells good, pour the glühwein in five 6-oz. cups. As you pour, murmur words like "Courmayeur" (offbeat Italian ski mountain), "Alice Kaier" (early den mother of U. S. women's ski racing) or "Geiger" (Swiss pilot who flies rich skiers onto high glaciers).

CHEESE FONDUE
By Guido, of Guido's restaurant in Aspen

1 lb. coarse-grated Swiss cheese
2 oz. kirsch
1 teaspoon cornstarch
2 globs chopped garlic
2 cups dry Swiss white wine
Salt, pepper (fresh ground)

Put wine, garlic, salt, pepper in pot and warm it — do *not* boil. Slowly add cheese, stirring constantly with wooden spoon. The instant all the cheese is melted, stir in the kirsch and cornstarch, which you have previously blended together. Bring up to — but not beyond — a boil, and serve. The entire operation must be smooth, easy, and sure. Never, but *never,* turn your back on cooking fondue. An untended fondue, like an untended woman, will swiftly turn into a blob; the good elements will separate, and the delicate flavor will be gone.

CHAPTER 28

LOW FASHION

Perhaps the most haphazard thing about the whole spontaneous evolution of American skiing has been ski fashion. When the sport first began in the Sierra (left), there was no such thing as fashion, for either youngsters or grownups. You simply put on whatever seemed likely to keep the weather out; usually, it didn't. The idea of being chic never occurred to anyone. When it finally did, the first attempts at fashion (see following pages) were worse than the earlier efforts to avoid it. Then came Mrs. Maria Bogner, and fashion suddenly became almost as important as snow.

Aspen, which now holds more chic women than any other ski resort, showed little promise as fashion center 80 years ago, when picture below was taken.

CIRCA 1910

In early 1900's, ladies began to show a touch of ankle, but still looked like impoverished Gibson girls.

1929   *Function began to overtake tradition, but no*

one had yet gotten around to designing for skiing.

1937

First fashions bloomed—but just barely—in Sun Valley. Pants and jackets matched, cap shielded eyes.

1938

This was the wool era, when girls tried to look cuddly. After a fall, they acquired crust of snow.

1939

Then came the button era, which slowed down the dressing process, but pioneered idea of snug fit.

1940

Then someone decided girl skiers would look more feminine in skirts. Happily, this idea died swiftly.

1940–50

During war decade, silhouette became slimmer, fabrics featured hard finish to shed snow, keep out wind.

The Look: Baggy to Bogner

One day in the winter of 1951, Arlene Dahl, on a visit to Sun Valley, proudly smoothed herself into what she thought were the very latest, most expensive ski clothes — gabardine pants, a skirted parka with pockets and fuzzy collar, a peaked cap, and all the accessories. Then she issued forth onto the slopes, and discovered that her gilt-edged wardrobe *was* late, all right. In fact, it was obsolete. Standing right next to her was Mrs. William Winans, of Beverly Hills, Calif., whose lower half had been poured into the smoothest, sleekest, most decidedly unbaggy pair of ski pants ever seen in the U. S. Mrs. Winans' slim, tight pants were hand-tailored in Europe to her own specifications, i.e., no droops or folds.

Being a trouper, Miss Dahl bravely posed with her adversary for a single, historic picture (left); then she burst into tears, junked her entire outfit, and built a new ensemble (total cost: $250) around a pair of slim pants, feeling, in the meantime, badly upstaged.

She wasn't the only one. American designers had been caught with a tradition — not to mention several bulging warehouses — of floppy pants. Still, the old-fashioned manufacturers managed to hold out for a couple of years. Then, four years after Arlene Dahl suffered her setback in Sun Valley, another debacle occurred on the same terrain. A lovely, prematurely white-haired German woman slithered into the Sun Valley Lodge. Many men followed to get a look. Many more women followed to ask the woman where she had gotten those adorable pants.

"I made them," said Maria Bogner. And indeed she had. She was — and still is — the head designer and stylist in her husband Willy's 500-man Munich ski-wear factory. Maria's pants were not just cut well. They were made from a

continued

Worst surprise in fashion history was suffered by Arlene Dahl (baggy pants) who sank fortune in old style, then encountered slim silhouette pioneer.

Best surprise was the hand-tailored, form-fitting coverall stretch suit, modeled at right by Mrs. Maria Bogner, the goddess-mother of modern ski fashions.

270

Quilted parka with roll-down hood replaced mackinaws and belted gabardine horrors of the 1940's.

brand-new fabric, a smooth, elasticized material that turned the already clinging pants into a sort of ankle-length bikini. As any fool could plainly see, this was the fabric of the future in skiing, and Maria, besides being beautiful, was no fool.

The year of the Dahl debacle, a French weaver of high-fashion silk had dropped into a converted sauerkraut plant where the Bogners had set themselves up in the ski clothing business. From a Swiss-patented fabric of kink-nylon Helanca and wool yarn, the Frenchman had made a sample pair of ski pants. "I liked the idea immediately," Maria told *Sports Illustrated* writer Roy Terrell, "I saw the possibilities. So we decided to take a chance."

That first year the Bogners put only 5 per cent of their production into stretch pants, but by 1955 they were making ski pants of almost no other material. As skiers worked up the courage to try stretch pants, they discovered the new fabric not only looked better, but performed better than anyone thought it would. The four-way give made the snug Bogners far more comfortable, especially in the knees, where old-style material tended to pull. The slick, close-woven stretch

continued

Soft, turtle-necked sweaters and matching ear-bands became favorites for ski and après ski about 1958.

Shaggy caps are warm, popular headpiece, make striking topper for high-collared black stretch suit.

pants were warm, and shed snow like an otter. If there was any noticeable sag after a wet day on the hill, it disappeared with a routine trip to the cleaner. Finally, the Bogners had replaced the blacks and browns traditional to ski wear with an eye-filling variety of reds, yellows, greens, purples, and even white.

Today the Bogners sell about 100,000 pairs of pants — and Maria's personal favorite, an overall stretch suit — to customers all over the world. Ingrid Bergman wears them. So do the Shah of Iran and the Swedish princesses and Toni Sailer and the Aga Khan. Almost every national ski-racing team in Europe wears Bogners — and those who do not have Bogners wear stretch pants by rival manufacturers.

Maria's only fear now is that someone is going to stretch things too far. "At first our pants were tighter in the leg than anyone else's," she told Terrell. "So others began to make them tighter. Now stretch pants are getting so tight as to be indecent. There is a point beyond which you should not go."

While rivals are groping to that point, Americans are grabbing at Bogners. Each year, 40 per cent of all Bogner pants are shipped to the U. S., to the delight of the manufacturer. "American girls are the best advertisement Bogner could have," said Willy, by no means oblivious to the dividends of flattery. "American girls have longer legs than Europeans and they look better in stretch pants. For export to America, we cut the pants longer, a special size."

"We cut them longer in back, too," says Maria.

"Yes," says Willy, "Your American girls are often much trimmer, you know, in what you call — uh — the behind. American girls are built like pears, European girls are more like apples."

Emilio Pucci slipped fine Italian hand into ski wear, came up with chic silk print jacket (upper left).

More practical — as ski clothes must be — and just as pretty are long-waisted sweaters worn in layers.

For après ski, anything goes, if you can afford it. Example, snow leopard and red fox parka (left), $875.

Another example for après ski, or no ski: tight, stretchy overalls at right, bound to create a following.

275

...And Back to Bogner Again

Although it is not immediately evident from the picture at left, below, the first true ski fashions were designed for men, about 1930. The man in the picture is Ernie Blake in his first incarnation as a skier, when he was a guide in his native Switzerland. His upper garment was the rage among ski pros of the time, a kind of double-breasted pre-Eisenhower jacket with a lot of cleavage in front. If the wearer was rich (no ski guide was), the jacket would be gabardine; otherwise it would be corduroy, or even a close-knit sort of canvas. The pants, which looked like ankle-length knickers, were also gabardine for the rich, corduroy for the rest. This was the costume the Alpine guides like Blake, Sig Buchmayr, and Hans Hauser brought over with them when skiing first began to grow in the U. S. But American males, always a little gun-shy about high fashion, ignored it for the type of makeshift outfit shown below on broadcaster Lowell Thomas at Franconia, N. H., in 1940. With only slight variations (like taking off the cap and getting socks inside the pants), this is what men wore until Bogners burst onto the scene. Then the men started getting very sleek indeed, the sleekest of all being young Willy Bogner, slamming through a slalom gate, at the right, in his own coverall stretch outfit.

First ski fashions for men appeared in Europe in the 1930's, were light, warm, functional and, compared to women's costumes of the day, quite chic. Less chic were outfits worn by U. S. pioneers like Lowell Thomas (above), whose bulky clothes weren't very warm. Latest in men's fashions is stretch suit (right).

276

CHAPTER 29

BEAUTIFUL BORE

After a man has been skiing about five years, if he happens to go out West or to Europe, someone will come smiling up to him and ask, "Would you like to go touring tomorrow?" If the man happens to have been a week-end skier for less than five years, he should instantly say, "No," and vanish into the bar. Because to answer "Yes" to this question implies that he has (1) strong legs for the seemingly endless climbing and traversing (left) on the trackless slopes that will be encountered at some terrible hour like seven the following morning; (2) good wind for the altitudes (right) that he will reach; and (3) nerves that will tingle happily rather than vanish altogether on such hairy slopes as those shown on pages 280–281. So much for basic equipment. An affirmative answer also implies that the skier can handle crust, slush, deep powder, and maybe even bare spots, since this is what one finds in spring when touring is best. And finally it implies he has some respect for the heights where he is going, and will not cut across an avalanche slope, thus burying himself or his friends forever.

Let us say that, contrary to all common sense, he says "Yes." One of two things will then happen. Either he will, on the tour, become exhausted, fall all over himself, hold up the whole party, and quit all skiing for good in a fit of understandable rage; or he will become exhausted, fall all over himself, hold up the whole party, and love every second of it, becoming forever after a Touring Bore.

A Touring Bore is like a Cruising Schooner Bore, or a Court Tennis Bore or a Stutz Bearcat Bore. He loves his difficult, time-consuming hobby with a single-mindedness that nonlovers find un-

continued

Anti-touring skiers find beauty of fresh snowfields spoiled by pain of breaking trail over miles of snow.

After climbing to a ridge no week-end skier would dream of approaching, a Touring Bore starts down.

278

Just under the summit of Mt. Hood, two Timberline instructors start a 6-mile descent over spring snow.

bearable. He is absolutely certain, as he will inform you over three hours of hot buttered rum, that his way of experiencing the sport is the only true way, and that all others are illegal, or immoral. And he is absolutely right.

The author, who has weak legs, poor wind, is yellow, cannot handle crust, slush, or powder (but is quite good on bare spots), is a Touring Bore, and has been ever since 1955, when he made an ass of himself during his first easy tour in the Bernese Oberland. Friedl Pfeifer, who has all the positive skier's attributes the author lacks, is a Touring Bore. It is the misty-eyed conviction of this otherwise tough and practical man that a chain of touring cabins would make big money around Aspen. Willy Schaeffler is a Touring Bore. So are Dick Durrance and his wife Miggs. So, also, is the author's sister, Kitty Prince, the tiny spot of human life below the rock spire on page 279. So is 1959 North American Ladies' champion Beverly Anderson, who, at the height of the competition in Squaw Valley, said, "The heck with the race. I'd like to climb down the back of KT-22 and get a little of that powder."

Later in summer, climbers and ski mountaineers rope up and pick way through glacial crevasses.

CHAPTER 30

G'WAN, SISSY

Every skier has the urge to show off. Depending on how shy or how good he is, this urge may be buried deep within or bubbling well above surface. For a pretty girl, it is easy. She simply pours herself into the right stretch pants and learns to lean charmingly on her poles or lounge lazily by the fire. For a man, unfortunately, showing off requires some action and not a little risk. The novice who clamps his feet together and hopes he can pull off a shortswing wiggle has one sure destination: flat on his face, having caught the outside edge of one ski. The same for the intermediate who decides deep powder looks easy; and the advanced week-ender who chooses to follow some young racer·in a fast ride through the moguls. But, despite the thuds of falling bodies and shrieks of the wounded, no skier ever stops trying. Nor should he. First of all, showing off is fun. Second, the only way to learn to ski better is to try something a little harder. It is not necessary to try anything as gracefully suicidal as Stein Eriksen's high-speed somersault, shown right at the instant after take-off when Stein goes into a swan dive layout. But a mild *geländesprung,* a flourishing stop-turn (sometimes called a liftline turn), or a gentle foray into the powder will, if tried often enough, eventually make you a better all-around skier. Besides, there is always the 20-to-1 chance it will work the first time, and the 200-to-1 chance that the proper person will be watching.

282

CHAPTER 31

PEANUTS

On skis, as elsewhere, kids seem to have more fun than anybody, and to look more appealing doing it. As with grownups, part of the fun is a chance to show off. For example, young Dick Durrance (top), though momentarily horrified at finding himself airborne, was the proudest kid in Aspen when he landed on his feet. That was ten years ago. Today, he is still landing on his feet and still enjoying it. In 1962, though only a freshman at Dartmouth, he was perhaps the finest skier in the college, a fact demonstrated when he placed second to all comers in the National Four-Way (downhill, slalom, cross-country, and jumping) championships at Heavenly Valley, Calif. Elsewhere across the country, other, smaller kids were having kicks of their own. In Sun Valley, tiny blonde Melanie Wilderman, an instructor's daughter, lit up like a Christmas tree when she discovered that, suddenly, she could stand up alone. In Seattle, a very young racer (No. 17, right) had the double pleasure of being a winner and a pretty little girl. Of course, it isn't always easy all the way. Out in Steamboat Springs, Colo., another tiny youngster (upper right) experienced that moment of universal doubt when, worn out and slightly lost in the shuffle, he began to wonder if it was all worth while. Turned out it was.

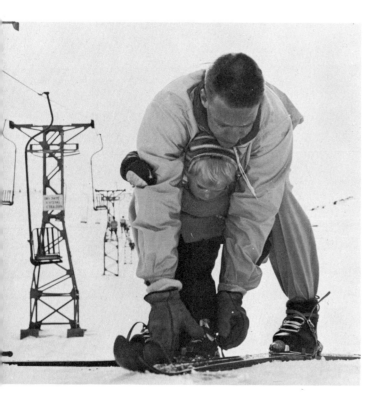

...And Their Hopeful Parents

There are only two ways to prevent a child from enjoying a ski trip. One is to let him get too cold, as Glenn Springer-Miller warned in Chapter I, but that is easy to avoid. Just send him indoors when he is wet, or when he is tired. The other way is to tell him that skiing WILL BE FUN, if he will only get OUT THERE and try harder! This is not so easy to avoid, especially if the parents love to ski, and the youngster is a squirming second-grader who would rather play cowboy. The solution? It is hard to find. But as a starter, heed Mrs. Springer-Miller's words that the only reason for a child to ski is to have fun on his own terms. *Not* on your terms. A doctor in Westport, Conn., said recently that his greatest pleasure from skiing is the close contact it has brought him with his teen-age son. This is a marvelous achievement, but it takes a lot of doing, not all of it too fascinating for the parents. One of the hardest things is to let the child make his own start — like playing cops and robbers on skis, if he wants. Then, like the father at left, you have to be around to help whenever the child needs it — which, at first, is all the time. Be ready to demonstrate a snowplow or a rudimentary turn (right, top) when asked, which will not be very often. And, if your legs and wind are good, try giving them a short piggyback or rucksack ride once in a while. Then, if everything goes just right, in about twenty years you will receive the one dividend of this long investment, when a large, blasé creature that used to be very small and belong to you, asks if you would like to go skiing tomorrow.

Seventy-four-year-old Herbert Butler (right) gave skiing a try, found it interfered with his night life.

Dr. William Milliken took it up 24 years ago at 50, has just served as President of Sun Valley Ski Club.

CHAPTER 32

SKI LIFE BEGINS AT 70

There is a popular impression, based on shudder-ing memories of plaster casts seen long ago, that skiing is strictly for the young. Consider, now, the gentlemen on these pages. At upper left, we have Dr. William Milliken, 74-year-old director emeritus of the Cleveland Museum; each winter he skis at Sun Valley for a solid month. At lower left is George Rengaard, of the Anchorage, Alas-ka, Ski Club; his age is kept a well-guarded secret, probably to avoid embarrassment to the youngsters who can't keep up with him. At top is Herbert Butler, who took up skiing in 1959 at the age of 74, then eased off, not because he sat down in the snow occasionally, but because he had a new young wife with whom he wanted to learn South American ballroom dancing.

George Rengaard, of Anchorage, Alaska, takes colt-ish leap as he warms up for a fast schuss *on slopes.*

Their spryness on the slopes is part of a trend among senior citizens to avoid decay by the pleas-ant means of going out and having fun. The chances of injury to these septuagenarians is less than to a *schuss*-booming teenager. An insurance survey conducted some five or six years ago proved that if a skier is over 21 and has taken 10 or more lessons, he can ski regularly for 14 years before he is likely to so much as sprain an ankle. And if he is wise enough to quit by three o'clock each day he may never get hurt at all. Dr. Milliken follows all these rules. He took his 10th lesson 23 years ago, quits every day at noon for a swim and a massage, and gets in condition each fall by 6-mile walks in the museum gardens. "It's a great feeling to stand on top of Baldy," he says, "and look down to the bottom. I made it twice last year without stopping. It gives you a sense of well-being—a sense of power." Of which, much more, to Dr. Milliken and all the rest.

CHAPTER 33

BIG DADDY
OF THE CARNIVALS

Photographs by Jerry Cooke

Gay Twenties party, with bathtub gin and clutch dancing, was feature of carnival in winter of 1955.

Modern hero in long line of great Dartmouth skiers is Chiharu Igaya, who won Olympic silver medal.

Real heroes of carnival are students and dates whose stamina carries them through 72-hour binge.

The ice statue, at left, presiding over the Dartmouth Winter Carnival is, by right of birthplace and lineage, the godfather of all snow carnivals. For the Dartmouth carnival, inaugurated 52 years ago, was the first of the nation's modern feasts to winter. In 1911, the year of its birth, the Dartmouth carnival was a tiny intramural affair that included beer guzzling, and some ragged events like snowshoeing and ski relay races. Today, the carnival is a wild, three-day round of intercollegiate ski races, hockey meets, swimming, basketball, beauty contests, dancing, beer drinking, cocktail drinking, bathtub gin drinking, and party, party. Other colleges have since taken up the idea, but it will be a cold day before any other school can match the Dartmouth week end.

Photographs by Bob Bourdon

...And His Various Offspring

Plaster-cast casualty spoofs risks of skiing, while top-hatted phantom announces that Stowe tops all resorts.

From Dartmouth the idea for a winter carnival spread to other colleges, and then to isolated towns like Steamboat Springs, Colo., where a few laughs in midwinter were more than welcome. Finally, it spread to resorts, where a new attraction amid the failing snow and failing customers of spring was also welcome. One of the better resort carnivals from the point of view of creating both laughs and late season business has been the annual Easter do at Stowe, shown on these pages.

Pseudo-Tyroleans give it the old oom-pah-pah in not very close harmony. At end of carnival, two young-

sters, disguised as horse or St. Bernard or something, receive prize from master of ceremonies Charles Black.

Photograph by Ernie Blake

CHAPTER 34

ULTIMATE THRILL

At the end of World War II a veteran of the 10th Mountain Division tried to put into words the extraordinary joy and excitement of a fast run in fresh powder. "It is the nearest thing to flying," he said; "it is almost a sexual feeling." Now this man was just back from the hill fighting in Italy, and therefore should be given a certain leeway. In the intervening years, he has doubtless had a chance to re-evaluate life's pleasures. Let us hope so. For fresh powder, like everything else, falls a good deal short of perfection. Nevertheless, it is something very special, not at all far from flying. It is a chance to wheel and swoop over the fastest, softest, safest surface imaginable.

But not at first. The first time it is a chance to make a complete, frightened, floundering idiot of yourself, with your skis locked in two deep, separate grooves that show no promise of ever coming together. All control is lost. You fall forward, backward, sideways. Each time, it takes half an hour to get up. There seems no reason for any sane person to go on doing this, and no hope that you will ever do it properly. Then, one miraculous day, you suddenly finish a turn on your feet. And then another, and another. Then your feet come together, and your skis pop up on top of the snow and, by God, you're doing it. And for the rest of your life you will never be truly happy skiing in anything but a fresh fall of deep powder.

Ringed by a halo of light from camera lens, a skier at Taos trails a luminous plume of light powder.

294

At Aspen, Friedl Pfeifer charges over the top of a ridge and makes a dramatic jump with the eye of the sun directly behind him.

Sometimes, as in the wide-open bowls behind Baldy at Sun Valley (right), the powder is so deep that half the skier disappears.

296

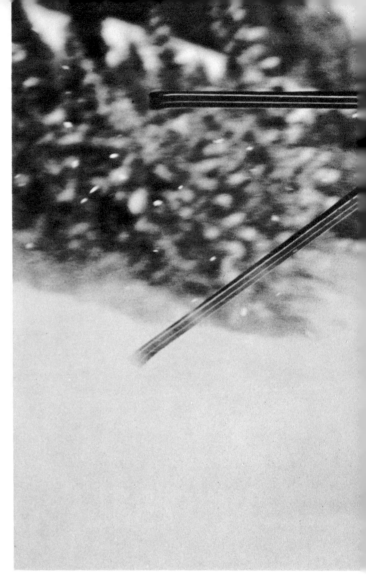

CHAPTER 35

ULTIMATE THUD

And now, in our waning pages, it is time to be honest. Skiing is not all deep powder and laughs. Sometimes the roads are icy. Sometimes the lift-lines are long. Sometimes the wind howls right through your bones. And sometimes, in fact a lot of times, you fall down. Even if you are Stein Eriksen (below), you fall down. Then you have only one recourse. Get up — and fall again.

298

THE
END

(But turn the page, anyway)

THE BEST

In eight years of traveling as Ski writer and Editor for *Sports Illustrated*, the author has gathered the following strictly personal impressions of who and what represent the very finest in American Skiing:

RESORT (chic)	*Aspen*
RESORT (folksy comfort)	*Big Mountain, Alta Lodge*
RESORT (special flavor)	*Taos*
MOUNTAIN (skiing)	*Ajax at Aspen*
MOUNTAIN (beauty)	*Baker — when you can see it*
TRAIL (hairy)	*High Rustler, Baldy Chutes, The Headwall*
SLOPE (practice)	*Bromley, Dollar Mt.*
SKI SCHOOL (beginners)	*Sun Valley, Bromley*
SKI SCHOOL (intermediates)	*Aspen, Stowe*
INSTRUCTOR (beginners, kids)	*Frank Day*
INSTRUCTOR (advanced)	*Conrad Staudinger, Karl Fahrner*
INSTRUCTOR (fun to ski with)	*Pepi Gabl*
INSTRUCTOR (technician)	*Paul Valar*
SKIER (packed snow)	*Stein Eriksen*
SKIER (off trail)	*Junior Bounous*
COACH	*Willy Schaeffler*
COMPETITOR	*Andrea Mead Lawrence*
SKI (expert)	*Kneissl White Star*
SKI (beginner, intermediate)	*Head Standard*
LODGE (comfort, service)	*Smuggler's Notch, Sun Valley*
PARTY TOWN	*Aspen*
PARTY SPOT	*Ski Club Ten*
SNOW	*Alta, Taos*
BEST DRESSED	*Miggs Durrance, Ann Taylor*

PHOTO CREDITS

Credits are separated from left to right by commas, from top to bottom by dashes. On page credits are given wherever display, layout, and logic permit. The author offers no defense for this system beyond his most sincere gratitude and good will to all the photographers herein represented.